Winter Glory

A Comedy

Peter Coke

Samuel French – London
New York – Sydney – Toronto – Hollywood

Copyright © 1988 by B.O.S. Ltd
All Rights Reserved

WINTER GLORY is fully protected under the copyright laws of the British Commonwealth, including Canada, the United States of America, and all other countries of the Copyright Union. All rights, including professional and amateur stage productions, recitation, lecturing, public reading, motion picture, radio broadcasting, television and the rights of translation into foreign languages are strictly reserved.

ISBN 978-0-573-01674-5

www.samuelfrench-london.co.uk

www.samuelfrench.com

FOR AMATEUR PRODUCTION ENQUIRIES

UNITED KINGDOM AND WORLD
EXCLUDING NORTH AMERICA
plays@SamuelFrench-London.co.uk
020 7255 4302/01

Each title is subject to availability from Samuel French,
depending upon country of performance.

CAUTION: Professional and amateur producers are hereby warned that WINTER GLORY is subject to a licensing fee. Publication of this play does not imply availability for performance. Both amateurs and professionals considering a production are strongly advised to apply to the appropriate agent before starting rehearsals, advertising, or booking a theatre. A licensing fee must be paid whether the title is presented for charity or gain and whether or not admission is charged.

The professional rights in this play are controlled by Film Rights Ltd in association with Laurence Fitch Ltd, 11 Pandora Road, London NW6 1TS.

No one shall make any changes in this title for the purpose of production. No part of this book may be reproduced, stored in a retrieval system, or transmitted in any form, by any means, now known or yet to be invented, including mechanical, electronic, photocopying, recording, videotaping, or otherwise, without the prior written permission of the publisher. No one shall upload this title, or part of this title, to any social media websites.

The right of Peter Coke to be identified as author of this work has been asserted by him in accordance with Section 77 of the Copyright, Designs and Patents Act 1988.

CHARACTERS

Dame Beatrice Appleby DBE ("Bee")
Dolores
Miss Nanette Parry ("Nan")
Miss Elizabeth Hatfield ("Hattie")
Brigadier Albert Rayne CB, CMG, MVO
Mrs Honeywell
Mrs Coyle
Fay Lombard
Sergeant Waller (non-speaking)
Bert (non-speaking)

The action of the play takes place in the sitting-room of Dame Beatrice's flat overlooking the Albert Hall

ACT I Scene 1 A morning in winter
       Scene 2 The following Sunday. Early afternoon

ACT II Scene 1 Ten days later. Afternoon
       Scene 2 Some weeks later. Afternoon

Time — the present

ACT I

Scene 1

The delightfully over-crowded and old-fashioned sitting-room of Dame Beatrice's flat overlooking the Albert Hall in London. Morning

Large french windows; a door to the hall; and another door to her bedroom

Dame Beatrice, well advanced in age, but with a bubbling personality and enthusiasm, is sitting having her hair brushed out by Dolores, a lovely extrovert with flamboyant clothes and hair, and a slight cockney accent, aged about twenty-five. The curlers and rest of her apparatus are on a table nearby

The telephone rings

Dolores Shall I?
Bee Uum—no, dear, thank you. I think it may be something a little—difficult. Call Nan, will you? Miss Parry.
Dolores (*going to the hall door; calling*) Miss Parry.
Nan (*off*) What is it?

Nan appears in the doorway. She is elderly, awkward, with a severe hairstyle, and a gruff manner which only partly hides her great kindness

(*Crossly*) I'm in the middle of writing a stinker to the Minister of Agriculture and Fisheries.
Bee Can he wait? (*She gestures to the phone*)
Nan (*crossing to it*) Of course.
Bee If it's you know who, you know what.

Nan nods, and picks up the phone

Nan (*speaking in a high and refined voice*) Hullo? Who is that? ... Oh, no, I'm sorry, but Dame Beatrice has gone to Zimbabwe.... Zimbabwe! Isn't it a lovely name? Redolent of their jungle and war-cries, don't you think? ... I really couldn't say; it depends on the weather and the Duchess.
Bee (*in a whisper*) Don't overdo it.
Nan (*on the phone*) The Duchess, her hostess.... I'll tell her immediately she gets back from (*dramatically*) Zimbabwe. (*She puts down the phone*) That should put him off for a bit.
Bee Thank you so much, dear. (*To Dolores*) Nan used to be—(*hastily correcting*)—Nan is—one of the most accomplished teachers of elocution in the country. So she's marvellous on the telephone.
Dolores The landlord?

Bee (*nodding*) How clever. He's a dreadful old fusser: we're only a few weeks overdue.
Dolores Fancy knowing a duchess.
Bee I don't. She's a duchess of the imagination, dear. One of the few things we do have a lot of in this house.
Dolores Oh, what a shame!
Nan (*looking at her*) I could do something about your vowels if you'd let me.
Dolores My——?
Bee (*clearly*) Vowels, dear.
Dolores Oh, I get it. (*Good-naturedly, to Nan*) And I could do something about your hair if you'd let me.
Nan (*grimly*) Touché. But, in my case, vanity's as short as cash, thank you.

She goes out

Dolores (*brushing again*) She's a one.
Bee Wait till you see the others.
Dolores I met Miss Hatfield: I did her hair.
Bee Of course you did: I get muddled. Then there's only the Brigadier. He won't want his hair done!
Dolores Have they always lived with you?
Bee Well, since my beloved husband died, about twenty years ago. Financially it was sensible for all of us.
Dolores What about the other flat next door with the old girls?
Bee You're very curious this morning?
Dolores Sorry; it's because I usually have to make clients talk so they don't notice if I cut off the wrong bit.
Bee The "old girls" next door are there because—in a rather extraordinary way which I'm not going to tell you, or you could get us all locked up—we made a lot of money. So we rent that flat for four people who deserve nice homes but can't afford them.
Dolores They're very lucky.
Bee We have two dear old sisters who think so. And a very nice new woman we've hardly met. But not a ghastly old horror we wish we never had met——

A tap on the door, and Miss Hatfield hurries in. She is old, small, sweet, and is always very highly strung

Hattie I must come in ...
Bee Yes, of course, Hattie dear. What is it?
Hattie Something most important. (*She stands with her hand to her mouth*) And I haven't any idea what! (*Tearfully*) Oh, it's awful: it's always happening. I rush to do something: then can't remember what it is. I'm really beginning to wonder about myself.
Bee Nonsense. I do it constantly. So long as it's not—(*numbering them off on her fingers*)—the bath running, something left on the gas, or an article of clothing not put on, there's nothing to worry about.

Act I, Scene 1   3

Hattie No, it's none of those—(*suddenly anxiously feeling over her body*)—I hope ...
Bee You know Dolores, don't you?
Hattie Yes.
Dolores I'm not suggesting anything, but isn't it time we had another appointment, Miss Hatfield?
Hattie (*awkwardly*) I'm not coming to you again ...
Dolores I thought I made you look fabuloso.
Hattie You insulted me.
Dolores You're thinking of someone else.
Hattie I'm not: you refused to let me pay. I know I'm only a poor china-restorer, who doesn't get very much restoring nowadays. (*Getting upset*) But I'd have you know I was very good once, and earned a lot. And your action humiliated me. Deeply ...

She hurries out in tears

Dolores Oh, dear.
Bee Don't worry: she's in one of her states because she's had a nasty letter from the bank. But it does remind me, dear: you must let me pay you a bit more this time.
Dolores You'll have another humiliated in a moment.
Bee I know what other places ask, and it's wrong that you should do it at less than half.
Dolores I've masses of rich clients who I overcharge so it's all the same in the end. (*She starts to pack up*)

The Brigadier marches in. He is as old as the others but still has a military bearing and manner, and treats everyone as if they were recruits. But has such charm that he usually gets away with it. He carries a clip-board which is his constant companion

Brigadier Why aren't we having morning coffee?
Bee Because Mrs Honeywell hasn't brought it yet.
Brigadier Why not: it's due at eleven hundred hours. (*He looks at his watch*) It's now eleven o nine. And thirty seconds.
Bee She has a great deal to do with both flats to run, Bertie.
Brigadier She wouldn't be ten seconds late if she kept to the schedules I've drawn up for her.
Bee If she had time to fathom those she'd always be late. (*Forestalling his anger*) Why don't you let this clever girl have a go at those ducks' tails round the back of your neck, Bertie.
Dolores Like me to snip them off, Brigadier?
Brigadier No, I would not. Thank you.
Dolores I'm used to doing men. My present boy-friend says I'm absolute tops.
Bee Oh, how is he?
Dolores Oh, not the one I told you about last time. I've got Bob now. Much better. Absolutely gorgeous. Has the loveliest nose you've ever seen: sends shivers down me spine. So what about it, Brigadier?

Brigadier A female cutting my hair?
Dolores I'll do it at half what you pay your man. And no tip.
Brigadier Hmm. I'll consider it.

Hattie opens the door, and lets in Mrs Honeywell, who carries a tray of mugs. She is middle-aged and homely. Hattie follows her in

Mrs Honeywell Coffee up, everyone.
Brigadier About time, too.
Mrs Honeywell Oh, am I late?
Brigadier Thirteen minutes fifteen seconds late.
Mrs Honeywell Oh, is that all.
Brigadier All, woman! Don't you realize that means I'll be thirteen minutes fifteen seconds late throughout the day?
Mrs Honeywell (*calmly*) Then you'd better drink your coffee quick. But mind, because it's scalding.

She goes out as Nan comes in and takes a mug of coffee

Hattie (*approaching Dolores with a mug*) I do apologize about just now. All caused by my running out of nerve-tonic.
Dolores I'll drop some in if you give me the name.
Hattie How very kind, but I'll remember, thank you. (*She ties a knot in her handkerchief*) Oh, there's one already: I wonder what that's for? Have some coffee.
Dolores I won't, thanks. (*Finishing packing up*) I'm already late for my next appointment.
Brigadier Lack of planning, probably. I'll draw you up a schedule if you like.
Dolores (*going to the door*) Thanks: we'll have a nice talk about it as I cut your hair. Tra-la all ...

They reply

Dolores goes out

Brigadier (*as they settle down to their coffee*) Pretty girl. Nice to see someone with a figure again.
Bee Thank you! But she's also a surprisingly good girl: always helping people.
Hattie (*sighing*) If only we still could.
Nan After the last disaster we really couldn't go on.
Bee I don't agree.
Brigadier You've obviously forgotten that that garden-party lost forty-four pounds and forty-nine pence.
Bee Only because the wretched marquee collapsed.
Nan Because we were too old to organize it properly.
Bee Rubbish! We could still do anything. We have imagination, experience, enthusiasm——
Brigadier (*interrupting*) And rheumatism, arthritis, and lack of memory.
Bee (*strongly*) Strengths if we used them properly. Obviously suffering from

Act I, Scene 1 5

those disabilities, and (*touching her cheek*) with the wisdom of age only too obvious, no-one would ever believe it was us if we did something — spectacular.

Hattie (*worriedly*) Oh dear, I don't like it when you're in this mood: it always leads to something awful.

Mrs Honeywell opens the door

Mrs Honeywell Sorry, but Mrs Coyle from next door insists on seeing you.

Mrs Coyle pushes in. Mrs Honeywell leaves. Mrs Coyle is a very bad-tempered, odd-looking old woman, carrying a two-handled straw basket with a bit of blanket sticking out. She grumbles rather than talks

Mrs Coyle (*threateningly; indicating the basket*) Have just taken Heloise walkies.

Bee Oh?

Mrs Coyle Thought I'd tell you as I hear there've been nasty complaints. And for the information of the complainer, (*heavily*) or complainers, it's already the second time today.

She stumps out

Bee There's gratitude for spending more than we've got on a flat where she lives practically free.

Brigadier Old witch.

Nan And hardly "walkies" when she hauls the little beast about in that basket.

Hattie Oh, I'm afraid that's my fault. I had two, so I gave her one so that the porters wouldn't see Heloise. She's not supposed to have a dog in the block.

Nan She shouldn't hang on to such a sick old dog anyway. The vet's begged her to have it put down, but she just calls him a fool, and lets it suffer.

Hattie I know; it's cruel. It worries me a lot.

Brigadier (*waving his hand in front of his face*) It's really unpleasant now. Did you notice it when she came in?

Nan Who wouldn't. I met little Mrs Mackintosh in the lift this morning. She said it smelt (*with a strong Scots accent*) worse than the boys coming off the fishing-boats after a week at sea.

Mrs Honeywell opens the door

Mrs Honeywell Mrs Lombard from next door to see you now.

Brigadier It's like a railway station this morning.

Mrs Honeywell shows in Fay Lombard, and exits

Fay's careful make-up, and the remains of great beauty, disguise her considerable age. She still overwhelms with her exuberance and traces of grandeur. She exaggeratedly emphasizes at least one word in every sentence

Fay My darlings, you must forgive me for such a completely unscripted entrance!

Bee Not at all, come in. (*Gazing at her*) But what have you done? You look wonderful.
Brigadier Quite radiant, Mrs Lombard.
Fay "Fay", darlings, please! After your angelic kindness and sweetness in allowing me to live in that adorable flat you must all call me Fay. I beg!
Brigadier We shall consider it an honour, Fay.
Fay Oh, you darling man! I'm as blind as a bat so I wasn't absolutely certain before, but now I have a close-up view you're even more distinguished-looking than I thought.
Brigadier (*delighted*) How very kind.
Fay Though I didn't come to praise, but to boast. (*Ecstatically*) Because something staggeringly wonderful has happened.
Bee Tell us quickly.
Fay Well, you'll never have heard of me of course, but AEONS ago I had quite a little success on the stage.
Hattie But we do know, Mrs Lombard—Fay. When we heard you were coming I dashed off and looked you up in the Public Library.
Fay (*aghast*) Dear God—not my age?
Hattie There was nothing about that.
Fay Heaven is merciful after all.
Nan But a great deal of what a wonderful beauty you were, and a long list of all the plays you'd starred in.
Brigadier I remember—I have to admit a little vaguely now—how thunderstruck I was the once I saw you.
Fay Oh, you are all so sweet! (*Sadly*) But then I had my illness, and everything was quite abysmal and everyone forgot me. (*Cheering up*) At least I thought everyone had forgotten me. And then last week—never say the age of miracles is over—a management rang and wanted to see me.
Nan What an excitement!
Fay Almost too much, darling. But I flew down—after hours with my make-up box—and—believe it or not—(*dramatically*)—I'm going to make a come-back.
Hattie No!
Bee How wonderful.
Brigadier Congratulations.
Fay Not an enormous part of course, and as old as Methuselah's Mother, alas. But a most effective and touching little scene right at the end of the play, and the promise of a ravishing frock.
Brigadier I'm delighted for you, my dear.
Bee The nicest news I've heard for years.
Nan I'm almost jealous.
Hattie (*excitedly*) We shall come to see you even if it's only in the gallery.
Fay The gallery! I shall give you a box, of course. And supper at the Savoy afterwards. And lots of other little treats. We'll have enormous fun! But I must flee now: I'm on my way to buy a new coat.
Nan Is there no end to your excitements?
Fay It will be exciting actually, darling. Because I've no money to pay for it. But I can't go on appearing in this ghastly old rag at rehearsals. I'm

Act I, Scene 1

getting a quite staggering salary, so I'm sure the shop will be sensible.
Bee My old fur coat's good, if rather unfashionable. You're very welcome to borrow it.
Fay How angelically generous! Oh, you're all so kind and enchanting that it's quite overwhelming. I shall fly before the tears stream from my eyes. Bless you, my darlings!

She goes out

Hattie How terribly exciting.
Bee I'm amazed at the change that's come over her. I hardly recognized her. I thought she was rather a poor old thing. Now she's glamorous.
Nan Because she's involved again. (*Sighing*) Extraordinary the difference it makes.
Bee I find it rather upsetting.
Nan Why?
Bee Well, there she is—a woman of even nearer blowing out the candle than we are—rushing off to give enjoyment. While we sit here vegetating like a lot of old Brussels sprouts.

Mrs Honeywell comes in

Mrs Honeywell It's no good: I can't put up with it! I've bitten my tongue till it's almost off, but I must speak.
Bee What's the matter, Mrs Honeywell?
Mrs Honeywell Mrs Coyle's the matter, Dame dear. And that pathetic little Heloise.
Bee Oh dear, what is it now?
Mrs Honeywell I've told you before I don't like doing her room. In fact I dread it. It always smells. But today—I'm sorry to put it like this: it stinks.
Nan I'll brave her and tell her she's got to keep the window open so long every day.
Mrs Honeywell No, it's not the window, Miss Parry. It's the carpet.
Brigadier But didn't we have new wall-to-wall put down? I remember because the old carpet's still waiting to be taken away.
Mrs Honeywell You won't think it was ever new if you look at it now.
Hattie Heloise?
Mrs Honeywell (*nodding*) Heloise. And I don't like saying it any more than you'll like hearing it but—(*closing her eyes*)—it's not just Number One, but Number Two as well.
Brigadier Good God!
Mrs Honeywell To say nothing of the sick puddles.
Hattie But she takes it for walks.
Mrs Honeywell She never takes it for walks! I've watched her. She takes the miserable creature out of the basket for two minutes, but it's half-blind and can hardly stagger so it just sits there looking lost, and back into the basket she crams it. It never does anything; except on the carpet. It's disgusting. And I'm telling you quite frankly: I like you all, I like my work, and I don't mind being underpaid. But either you make her have it put down as it should be, or—I'm sorry to say it—no ifs and buts, I leave.

She goes out

They all sit rather stunned

Bee (*eventually*) I'm afraid we must make her put it down.
Hattie Oh dear, must we?
Bee Not just because we'd lose Mrs Honeywell. (*Strongly*) But because we can't be so feeble as to let that animal go on suffering.
Hattie Yes, poor little thing. It's always obviously in pain. But Mrs Coyle'll never agree.
Bee Then we must get round her non-agreement.
Nan It'd be difficult: she never lets that basket out of her sight.
Brigadier (*suddenly*) Basket! That's it.
Bee What's it?
Brigadier Didn't you say you had a basket like it, Miss Hatfield?
Hattie That I do my shopping in, yes.
Brigadier Bring it, will you?
Hattie If you want it ...

She runs out

Bee I think I know what you're at, Bertie.
Nan Take it into our own hands?
Bee (*thinking*) Some sort of a switch.
Brigadier Exactly. (*Thoughtfully*) If we plan it properly it might be quite easy.

Hattie hurries back with the basket

Hattie Your basket, Brigadier.
Brigadier Good. Now ... (*Writing on his clip-board, as he does on and off during the scene*) We don't want to wear gas-masks, so we'd better get her out of her room. And attack her in here.
Bee She's very greedy; shall we ask her to a meal?
Brigadier Good.
Hattie Won't she be suspicious when we've never had her all these months?
Nan We can say it's some sort of a celebration.
Bee And ask Fay, too, as camouflage.
Nan Have to be on a Sunday, then.
Brigadier Why?
Nan Otherwise she'll be at rehearsals.
Brigadier (*writing it down*) Good thinking. The plan's maturing.
Hattie (*plaintively*) Could someone explain exactly what we're planning?
Bee To get Mrs Coyle in here with Heloise in the basket. Then, Brigadier?
Brigadier Then ...? I've no idea. Could some of the rest of the Think-Tank think.
Nan (*thinking it out*) We have this second basket—which we must make look like the first basket ...
Brigadier Can you undertake that, Miss Hatfield?
Hattie You mean—an old piece of blanket sticking out like she's got, and then something heavyish inside it. Books?

Act I, Scene 1

Brigadier (*surprised*) Excellent, Miss Hatfield.
Hattie Oh, thank you, Brigadier.
Nan So now we have the two baskets——
Brigadier I shall refer to them in orders as "H" and "B".
Hattie You mean "A" and "B".
Brigadier (*provoked*) I do not mean "A" and "B", Miss Hatfield! I mean "H" and "B". "H" for Heloise, "B" for books. Is not that simpler?
Hattie Oh, yes, I suppose so. (*Murmuring to herself*) "H" for Heloise, "B" for books.
Brigadier Then we get "H" away from her, and substitute it with "B".
Nan (*nodding*) So she won't miss it.
Bee Next we have to get "H" out of the room.
Hattie Why?
Brigadier Well, we can't do it in front of her, can we?
Hattie What?
Brigadier (*exasperated*) Miss Hatfield, why are we forging this elaborate plan?
Hattie I'm sorry, but I really have very little idea.
Nan (*kindly to her*) We've got to get Heloise's basket out of the room, dear, so that the deed can be performed.
Hattie You mean we're actually going to——(*She pauses in horror*)
Brigadier (*firmly*) Yes.
Hattie Oh dear, do we really have to?
Nan It's a kindness, Hattie, you know it is.
Hattie Yes, I do, deep down. (*Convincing herself*) It really is only being merciful; it must suffer terribly. All right. (*Hastily*) So long as I have nothing to do with doing it.
Bee How are we going to do it by the way?

Pause while they all think

Nan The bath?
Hattie Oh, no: that'd be too ghastly.
Brigadier (*acidly*) Then what do you suggest, Miss Hatfield?
Hattie Well something more humane. And quick. Couldn't it be something instant?
Nan Overdose of pills of some sort?
Brigadier (*thoughtfully*) Instant pills . . . ? (*Suddenly jumping to his feet*) By Jove! I think I've got it . . .

He rushes out of the room

Hattie Oh, heavens! What's he got?
Nan (*slowly*) I have a horrid idea it's going to be his revolver.
Hattie Oh, no!
Bee No, we can't have shots being fired in the bathroom.
Nan If she hears bangs Mrs Coyle's going to know something's up.
Hattie Anyhow somebody might be shot! His hand's very shaky. The bullet might go into any of us.

Bee He'll be the only one there, dear. If he shoots himself in the foot—what am I saying? We must stop him at all costs.

The Brigadier comes back with his hands behind his back

Brigadier We're in luck: it's the very thing.
Hattie (*agitatedly*) It isn't, Brigadier! You're not to do it. We've all agreed.
Brigadier Now calm down, Miss Hatfield. You've no idea what I've got because I didn't know myself; I'd forgotten.
Nan It isn't a revolver, then?
Brigadier I threw my revolver from Waterloo Bridge to prevent my shooting Tony Benn.
Bee Then what is it, Bertie?
Brigadier For a time in the War I was Escape Officer. This meant I had possession of all escape devices. Such as tiny compasses hidden in shirt studs, files in pencils et cetera. (*Emphasizing*) It also meant I had the means to prevent anyone with highly classified knowledge from being taken alive.
Bee Oh, my goodness! Poison?
Brigadier Exactly. Instant working pills. Forgotten in the false bottom of my kit-bag all these years.

He shows a small tin of pills. Hattie draws back in alarm

Bee How d'you know they'll still work?
Nan Seeds from Tutankhamun's tomb sprouted after hundreds of years.
Brigadier What the hell's that got to do with it. Oh, yes, I see. Of course they'll work. (*Shuffling through his notes*) Now, where had we got to?
Nan Trying to find a way to get basket "H" out of the room.
Bee Difficult if she's watching.
Hattie How were we getting "B" into the room?

The Brigadier hectically searches his clip-board

Brigadier We seem to have missed that out.
Nan Damn.
Bee (*thinking*) The baskets must be hidden in something we can carry in and out. Wait a moment: I've got an idea ...

She hurries off into her bedroom

Hattie (*faintly*) What are we going to do with the—corpse?
Brigadier Dispose of it.
Hattie How?
Nan Easy. You and I take the basket—well weighed down with a rock——
Hattie Where do we get a rock in a flat?
Nan (*annoyed*) Well, not necessarily a rock; something weighty. That old flat-iron I prop my door open with.
Brigadier (*jotting it down*) Flat-iron provided by Parry.
Nan Then we go down to the Serpentine, and fling it in where it's nice and deep.
Hattie But suppose someone sees!

Nan (*after a moment's thought*) Look! (*She points up, and shouts excitedly*) Look!

The Brigadier and Hattie look anxiously to where she's pointing

Hattie What is it?
Nan A UFO.
Brigadier A what?
Nan A saucer. A flying saucer. Look at it—streaking across the sky.
Hattie I don't see anything.
Nan (*crossly*) Because you're not looking. While everybody else does, you sink the basket.
Hattie Oh, I see!
Brigadier Good thinking. (*He jots it down*)

Bee returns

Bee Can't find the damn thing. But I've got an even better idea if someone'll come and help me.
Hattie (*proudly*) We've got rid of the corpse.
Bee We don't want to get rid of the corpse.
Brigadier Of course we want to get rid of the corpse.
Bee We don't! If we do she'll know we've done it. She's got to find it in the basket. Then she won't be so upset as she'll think it happened naturally because of old age.
Nan I'm afraid that's perfectly right. Damn.
Brigadier Yes, it's messed up my orders. (*Crossly crossing out*) No flat-iron. No flying saucer.
Bee (*shaking her head incomprehensibly*) Come on, Nan ...

Nan follows her into the bedroom

Brigadier Perhaps it's not going to be quite as easy as I thought.
Hattie I'm sure it isn't. Should we cancel the whole thing?
Brigadier (*staring at her in amazement*) Suppose General Montgomery had cancelled his whole battle-plan on the eve of El Alamein?

Hattie looks mystified

See what I mean?

Before she has to answer Bee and Nan come on carrying a small tub chair

Nan Splendid idea, Dame Beatrice. Just the job, I'd say.
Brigadier Then perhaps you'll kindly say it to us, so that we can discuss it before I put it in orders and mess them all up again?
Bee It's simplicity itself, Bertie. At the luncheon we leave one place without anything to sit on. We suddenly "notice", and bring on this chair.
Hattie Beautifully clear so far.
Bee In the chair—covered by a cushion or a rug or something—is the false basket.
Brigadier Refer to it as basket "A", please.
Hattie (*puzzled*) Which is basket "A"?

Brigadier (*crossly*) The one with the books in. Oh, no, that's "B" for books, of course. (*Even more cross at his mistake*) Well, "B" or "A" or "A" or "B" or "B" and "H", it really doesn't matter.
Nan It does matter, Brigadier. We've got to get it clear or there'll be a muddle.
Bee (*hastily trying to pour oil on this troubled water*) It's all perfectly clear really. We bring in "B" basket, which is "a" basket, after all, which is what Bertie meant when he called it "A" basket, though of course it's really "B" basket. (*Despairingly*) Or is it "H" basket: I wish I'd never started this.
Nan (*taking control*) We bring "B" basket in, with a cushion over it. Then while someone causes a kerfuffle——
Brigadier (*correcting*) A diversion.
Bee I'll get on to the subject of what we're eating, and give her the recipe. Or in emergency spill wine.
Nan Perfect. Then while she's busy mopping, we snatch up the basket with the dog in . . .
Brigadier Basket "H".
Nan Put it in the chair . . .
Hattie And put the one already in the chair—basket "B" . . . ?
Brigadier Correct.
Hattie Then put that one down on the floor to take the place of the other.
Nan Precisely. Does that make sense, Brigadier?
Brigadier (*grudgingly*) Can't see any actual snags. (*Writing*) I'll get it down.
Bee Then it's quite easy to get the chair out again. We suddenly remember it's got a gammy leg, and remove it back to the bedroom.
Nan The Brigadier'll have to do that.
Brigadier Why me?
Nan Because you're the one who's actually got to—do the deed.
Brigadier Couldn't one of you do it?

They all say "No" together, very firmly

(*Resignedly writing*) Self: Administrator of Pill.
Hattie Will you know how to make her take it?
Brigadier I'm not half-witted, Miss Hatfield.
Hattie No, of course, but it's very difficult to give dogs pills. You have to stroke their throats to make sure they've swallowed it properly.
Brigadier This is not a pill for tape-worms, Miss Hatfield. It's deadly. One taste, and you're gone.
Bee Then the best thing would be to put it in a lump of raw meat.
Hattie Heloise hasn't got any teeth: she might never get to it.
Bee We'll mince it, then.
Brigadier In which case we'd better grind a pill into powder; then it'll mix in properly. (*Writing*) I'm putting down pestle and mortar.
Bee Then cross it out again: we haven't got one.
Nan A bottle, that's all that's needed. That's how I crunch up breadcrumbs.
Brigadier (*writing*) Bottle for Parry. Then I think we've got it all wrapped up.

Bee We haven't got the corpse back to her feet yet.
Brigadier Oh, my God, neither we have.
Hattie We can't bring it back in a chair we've already said is broken.
Nan No reason not to bring another chair, though.
Bee Yes: there's still a place without one.
Nan My TV chair's not a thing of beauty but deep enough to hide in. Shall I fetch it?
Bee No, we know you've got it.
Brigadier Though, wait a sec. It might be a wheeze to have it. Then we could rapidly do a dry-run of the whole operation, so that I can see we've not forgotten anything for Orders.
Nan Top-hole idea.

She hurries out

Hattie (*agitated*) We're going to go through it now?
Bee Just a sort of rehearsal, dear.
Hattie I really don't think I could manage it after two days of no nerve-tonic.
Brigadier Balderdash. You've really got nothing to do except dither about.
Hattie I shall manage that all right.

Nan comes back with her chair

Nan You may find a few toffee-papers. But I'll give it a good brush before the day.
Bee (*going to pick up her chair*) This'd better go back in my room.

Hattie rushes to help her

Brigadier Wait a sec! Wait a sec. We don't want everyone rushing about like hens turned off their nests. If we're to have success we must use a strict military procedure. Line up there where I can see you.
Hattie Can't you see us here, Brigadier?
Brigadier I want you where I can keep an eye on each of you all the time.

With sighs of resignation they line up

That's better. Now: Appleby and Hatfield place chairs in bedroom. Move!

Bee and Hattie, with two tub chairs, go into the bedroom

In the meantime you and I, Parry, place table in luncheon position. Move!

They take the table: pull up the flaps, and place it near the centre of the room

Hattie and Bee come back, and the three stand in line again

Now. Each place a chair in eating position. Move!

They each place a chair

Bee That only makes four. How many of us will there be?
Nan Us four, Mrs Coyle and Fay. Six.

Brigadier Two more chairs then.
Bee One more chair then. Remember we're bringing in one.
Brigadier (*crossly*) Exactly what I meant. One; then we're bringing in one: two.
Nan (*placing the fifth chair*) We'll put Mrs Coyle nearest the door so that there won't be so far to carry.
Brigadier Good thinking.
Bee (*moving the chair*) So the space must be next to her.
Brigadier Correct. Places!

The three line up again

Now: Equipment. (*Studying Orders*) The two baskets.
Hattie We've only one.
Bee Shall we use the waste-paper basket for Mrs Coyle's for now?
Brigadier Good. "B" basket to first chair, Hattie.

After moments of indecision Hattie seizes the basket and rushes off

"Flat-iron". No, we cancelled the flat-iron. "Poison meat": we can take that as already being in the bathroom.
Bee (*picking up the pills*) But we mustn't leave these lying about. (*Moving to the grandfather clock*) I'll put them where I hide the gin from Mrs Honeywell. (*She does so*)

Hattie comes back

Brigadier That seems to be about all. So we'll go ahead with Action. Wait! "H" basket had better be where Mrs Coyle'll have it. At her feet.
Nan (*placing the waste-paper basket*) About there?
Bee Yes, I should think that'd be all right. Shall we start from where we're all about to sit?
Brigadier Yes, no need for all the rubbishy social preamble. Luncheon places everyone. Move!
Bee (*gesturing; speaking in her "hostess" voice*) I think if you'll sit there, Fay dear. And I feel you'll be most comfortable there, Mrs Coyle. That's right: put little Heloise near you so that she'll be as happy as we all are.
Nan (*slightly falsely*) Oh, how silly!
Hattie What?
Nan We're one seat short.
Bee So we are! Perhaps you could find one from from my bedroom, dear?
Nan Of course.

She goes into the bedroom

Bee (*to the empty chair*) I do hope you're going to enjoy this first course. I got the recipe from a woman who knew a woman whose son knew a woman ... (*Shaking her head*) I'll work it out before the day.

Nan comes back with the first tub chair

Nan Would this one be all right, Dame Beatrice?
Bee Perfectly. Put it there would you, dear?

Act I, Scene 1 15

Nan places it, and sits next to it

(*Continuing to the empty chair*) You simply must try this recipe. Here's a piece of paper and a pencil. (*In her ordinary voice to the Brigadier*) Paper and pencil on list, Bertie.
Hattie I thought we were going to spill wine?
Bee We haven't got it yet, dear. (*To the Brigadier*) In fact that can be your excuse for going out, Bertie.
Brigadier (*jotting*) Bottle of wine.
Bee (*to the empty chair*) Now, dear. (*Giving a significant nod to Nan*) Four eggs, eight ounces or so of cream—double if you can afford it—an eight-ounce tin of salmon—and don't get the Russian: it's very nasty—a spoon of mayonnaise—home-made, of course, and the usual pepper and salt.

During this Nan has nimbly switched baskets and now stands up

Nan Good gracious!
Brigadier What is it?
Nan I've just noticed this chair is all wobbly. I'll change it.
Bee Do: we don't want an accident.
Brigadier Bless my soul: I've forgotten the wine. I'll give you a hand, Miss Parry, on the way.

They go out carrying the chair in which they've put the basket

Bee (*calling to them*) Come straight back for now: there's no point in us just chatting as there are only the two of us.

Nan comes back with the basket in the second chair. Followed by the Brigadier with a vase

Brigadier This'll have to do for the wine for now.
Nan (*placing the chair*) There: that's safer.
Brigadier I do hope you'll enjoy this wine, Mrs Coyle. Not very old, but has a most unusual bouquet.
Hattie I think it's delicious.
Brigadier (*crossly*) You haven't got any yet. (*To the empty chair*) Oh, I do apologize. I've spilt a drop or two on your dress.
Bee Oh, Bertie, how careless. Never mind, dear. If I sponge it with my napkin dipped in a little water—(*rubbing vigorously in the air*)—it shouldn't leave the slightest stain.

During this Nan has again deftly switched baskets

Nan (*getting up*) Oh, dear! Some of it's splashed on this lovely chair. I'll deal with it straight away: we don't want the velvet marked. (*She whisks the chair to the door, but leaves it there*) Operation completed!
Brigadier Bravo, everyone. A very commendable first attempt. If we go through it a few more times to iron out any——(*He breaks off as* . . .)

Mrs Honeywell comes in

Mrs Honeywell Getting the table ready a bit early, aren't you?

Bee We—we just thought we'd help you.
Mrs Honeywell I didn't mean you had to help me, Dame dear. I'm not work-shy. It's just that I cannot, and will not, put up with filth.
Bee We have got that message, Mrs Honeywell.
Mrs Honeywell So you'll do something about it?
Bee We will.
Mrs Honeywell And soon?
Bee And soon. In fact: next Sunday.

Curtain

Scene 2

The same, the following Sunday. Early afternoon

The table is laid for luncheon, with the chairs placed except for two. On one of these Nan sits astride with an open script in her hand. Fay lies on the sofa

Fay "... and what, may I ask, is this?"
Nan (*in a man's voice*) "Your pudding, Mother."
Fay "My pudding. I, who should be tempted with sliced nectarines floating in a pool of crushed raspberries and pomegranate seeds, am given: sago."
Nan (*in a man's voice*) "You want building up, Mother."
Fay "I'll tell you what I want." (*She pauses*) "I'll tell you what I want——" It's no good, darling, you'll have to tell me what I want.
Nan Sewage farm.
Fay Oh yes. "I want you——" uum—what's his name, darling?
Nan Sebastian.
Fay "I want you, Sebastian, and you——" now I can't remember his damn wife's name.
Nan Ghislaine.
Fay Ridiculous name. No wonder I can't remember it. I've asked them to change it to Marie or Jeanne or something simple but, no, it's got to be— what is it?
Nan Ghislaine.
Fay Ghislaine. Because it reflects her character! In which case they shouldn't have cast a girl who looks like a pancake with two currant eyes.
Nan "I want you Sebastian, and you Ghislaine ..."
Fay Oh, yes. "I want you Sebastian and you Ghislaine—(*acidly*) immediately you've finished this delicious sago—to pack your bags and drive off to your dreary little stucco villa near the sewage farm. (*Very firmly*) And stay there."
Nan (*with a French accent*) "You are cruelle, Madame. Sebastian, you must not let 'er speak to me like that." (*In a man's voice*) "No, you must not speak to us like that, Mother!"
Fay "For the first and only time I shall grant your wish (*through her teeth*) Ghislaine."
Nan (*French*) "What is it you mean, Madame?"

Fay "I mean—that from this moment—I am never, ever, going to speak to either of you again." And I exit.
Nan (*clapping*) Splendid. That was really lovely.
Fay Thank you, my saviour. Could you bear to go through it just once more?
Nan As many times as you like.
Fay Treasure! Just before we begin tell me Pancake's name again.
Nan Ghislaine.
Fay Ghislaine. (*She beats her forehead as she repeats the name over and over*)

Bee comes in carrying a decorated mousse on a dish

Bee Sorry to interrupt, but I'm afraid we must turn the rehearsal room back into a dining-room.
Fay Don't be sorry, my redeemer. You've rescued me from purgatory.
Bee How's it going?
Fay Owing to this darling girl, miraculously. I'm word perfect.

Hattie comes in with a small vase of flowers

Hattie I know it's extravagant, but as it's a celebration——
Fay Oh, no-one told me! What are we celebrating?

The other three look blank for a moment

Nan The Brigadier's birthday.
Fay Oh, I'd have brought him something had I known. Oh, wait a minute, I did bring something. (*Fetching a carrier-bag*) Instead of both being for you, do you mind if I give him one as a birthday offering?
Bee I'm sure he'll be delighted. Surprised maybe, but delighted.

The Brigadier comes in

Brigadier Twelve fifty-nine. Is everyone on Parade?
Fay Ah, here is the noble warrior himself. (*Giving one of the bottles of champagne to him*) Salutation and felicitation, brave soldier.
Brigadier Why are you giving me this?
Bee (*clearly*) It's a birthday present, Bertie.
Brigadier It isn't my birthday.
Hattie Now don't be naughty, Brigadier. You know perfectly well it's your birthday.
Brigadier Not for another two months.
Nan (*to Fay*) He always pretends it isn't his birthday. Vanity.
Bee (*very distinctly*) But it is your birthday, Bertie, or why would we be having this birthday celebration?
Brigadier (*getting the point at last*) I surrender: female cunning has defeated me. Thank you, dear lady, for your welcome and extravagant gift. (*Fetching another bottle*) And I thought I was being generous when I bought a bottle of rather indifferent sherry. (*Serving it*) Which I think we'll start——
Fay Oh, not for me, darling: I never drink at midday.
Brigadier Not just to please me?

Fay (*holding out her glass*) Pour out the whole bottle, tempter.
Brigadier (*looking at his watch*) Where's that damn woman? She's four minutes late already.
Hattie (*horror-stricken*) Suppose she's forgotten?
Fay No such hope. When I left she was putting on ghastly purple hat. That only comes out on "occasions".
Bee Oh dear, it sounds as if you're not very fond of her.
Fay My darlings, I absolutely detest her. I think she's a rude, malicious, ill-mannered, vulgar, boring and decidedly niffy old horror. I won't say more as it's Sunday.
Hattie (*refusing sherry*) Oh, no, thank you, Brigadier. But I think I'll have a little of my nerve-tonic. (*She goes to a small table, pours some out and swallows it*)
Fay Oh, my poor treasure. Are you feeling seedy?
Hattie No, no, not really. It's rather more—in case.
Fay In case of what, my little one?
Bee (*stepping in*) In case the meal's overcooked, I expect.
Brigadier It really is too bad: five minutes and thirty-five seconds now.
Nan Do you think I'd better telephone?
Hattie I have an awful idea she's not coming at all.

Mrs Honeywell comes in

Mrs Honeywell Mrs Coyle.

She shows her in and goes

Mrs Coyle is wearing the purple hat

Mrs Coyle (*grimly*) The *Daily Express* says its fashionable to be late. So, though hungry, I thought I'd be—(*scornfully*)—fashionable.
Fay But you are anyhow in that—outstanding hat.
Bee (*hastily*) Come in, Mrs Coyle. You know everyone.

They murmur greetings

Brigadier Some sherry, Mrs Coyle?
Mrs Coyle Never touch it. All those Spanish feet, and flies and lizards falling in.
Bee (*brightly*) Then, if you all agree, I think we'll start luncheon. (*Noticing*) Wait a moment! Where's Heloise?
Mrs Coyle Left her.
Nan But you never leave her!
Mrs Coyle Well, I have.
Hattie But why?
Mrs Coyle I recognize a wrinkled nose when I see one. And I've seen more than one in this flat.
Bee What nonsense. We were expecting her.
Brigadier We've got a little tit-bit all ready.
Hattie She's not used to being left alone; she'll be miserable.

Act I, Scene 2   19

Mrs Coyle She was.
Bee Then why not fetch her? We'd like to have her ... (*To the others*) We really would, wouldn't we?

All agree energetically except Fay

Mrs Coyle A surprise. But as I want her anyhow ...

She goes out

Fay Far be it from me to question your darling humanity, but why in God's name do you want that half-dead animal?

The others look at each other

Bee Well, you see——(*She stops in despair*)
Nan No, we'd better tell her. Rabies.
Fay But it can't possibly have rabies!
Nan No. But we have an idea it's met another dog smuggled in from France.
Fay No!
Brigadier Yes.
Bee So better safe than sorry: we've arranged for a vet to drop in "by chance" after luncheon.
Fay How wise.
Bee But for heaven's sake don't mention it——
Nan Or the whole plan could fail.
Hattie I only had a small tonic: I think I'll have a little more. (*As she's about to help herself ...*)

Mrs Coyle returns. She carries a bundle wrapped up in a blanket

Mrs Coyle The missing guest.
Bee Oh, good. Now I suggest you put her——
Hattie (*interrupting hectically*) But she's not in her basket!
Nan We thought she practically lived in her basket.
Mrs Coyle She does.
Brigadier Then why isn't she in it now?
Mrs Coyle It's a bit grubby.
Bee But if she's happier in it—who minds a little grubbiness?
Hattie (*breathlessly*) I'll fetch it, shall I?
Brigadier Good thinking, Hatfield.

Hattie rushes out

Mrs Coyle (*to the bundle*) All buzzing about like bees for you, my poppet. Isn't that a surprise?
Brigadier Well, let's get seated, shall we? Fay, we thought if you'd go there——
Fay How lovely.
Brigadier And you, Mrs Coyle, there——
Mrs Coyle No, I don't like the light in my eyes. I'll sit here. (*She plonks herself in the chair furthest from the door*)

Slight consternation

Brigadier But we'd planned for you to sit here.
Mrs Coyle (*not moving*) I can't keep getting up and down: I've got arthritis.
Brigadier (*getting angry*) We've all got arthritis——
Bee All right, Bertie, all right.
Nan It won't make all that difference, Brigadier. The slightest rethinking and all will be well.
Brigadier I wish I were as confident.

Hattie runs in with the basket and goes to the chair Mrs Coyle should be in

Hattie Here we are. Oh, no we're not! Why are you sitting over there?
Fay Perhaps because she doesn't want her wrinkles seen.
Mrs Coyle At least "she" doesn't spend hours attempting to fill the cracks with make-up.
Bee (*clapping her hands before Fay can answer*) Now, come along everyone, come along. The roast beef will be burnt to a cinder if we don't start.

They begin to take their places

Hattie (*holding out the basket*) There you are, Mrs Coyle: pop her in there.
Mrs Coyle (*doing so and glancing at Fay*) Yes, better for her not to hear her mother being insulted.
Hattie Then we'll put her down here, where you can keep an eye on her.

The others give her baleful looks as she puts the basket on the floor near Mrs Coyle

Bee (*fetching the mousse*) I do hope you won't mind, but the first course is cold. Not laziness, but because I was given the most exciting recipe.
Nan (*exclaiming loudly*) Oh!
Bee What is it?
Nan We've forgotten the sixth chair.
Bee Oh, how stupid. Someone fetch a chair from my bedroom, will they.
Brigadier I'll go.
Nan No, no that's my job! (*Covering up*) I mean: carrying's bad for your back.

She goes into the bedroom

Mrs Coyle You've got a bad back, too?
Brigadier (*overdoing feeling his spine*) War wound.
Mrs Coyle If you suffered a quarter of what I suffer——

Nan brings back the first tub chair

Oh, a chair with sort of arms. I'll find that much more comfortable.

As she struggles to her feet Nan whips out the basket hidden with a cushion, and hides it on the sofa

Bee No, no, don't move——
Mrs Coyle The specialist said I must have my arms supported when I'm sitting. (*She lowers herself into the tub chair*) Not comfortable, but better.

Act I, Scene 2   21

The others stare in consternation

Fay (*sitting very upright*) How lucky I am to be able to sit straight-backed without support.
Mrs Coyle If you knew what you looked like pretending to be at least thirty years younger than——
Brigadier (*loudly jumping in*) A new recipe, did you say, Beatrice?
Bee Yes. (*To Mrs Coyle*) If you find it as delicious as I think you will, I'll share the secret.
Mrs Coyle Useless. I can hardly stand long enough to boil an egg.

The others show slight consternation at this set-back

Fay Give it to me, darling. I shall receive it with the gratitude such a full-hearted offer deserves.
Bee (*serving it*) Better taste it first.
Fay Only a soupçon then, or I'll never get into my ravishing frock.
Mrs Coyle A nice large portion for me. Fortunately I don't have to exhibit myself on a stage.
Fay I'm usually a placid girl——
Nan (*getting up in imagined alarm*) Oh, I've just remembered. (*Going to Mrs Coyle's chair*) Isn't that the chair we put away because it had a wobbly leg?
Brigadier Bless my soul! You're right.
Hattie Quickly, Mrs Coyle, or you may have an accident.
Mrs Coyle Feels perfectly safe to me.
Nan If you had a fall on top of your present disability——
Mrs Coyle I'll risk it. I'm not wasting more energy playing musical chairs. I want my food.

She tucks in with gusto. The others watch alarmed, with Nan gesturing "What are we going to do?" behind her

Bee Sit down, and don't worry, Nan. (*Meaningly*) Inspiration comes if one just sits calmly. (*Noticing Mrs Coyle watching her*) As I always found when I was a writer.
Fay My darling: I never knew! You're a famous author. You must write me a play.
Mrs Coyle You'd have to write it very, very, quickly!
Bee (*seeing Fay about to explode*) I'm afraid I was boasting: it was mostly letters.
Fay And I was boasting, too. (*Pitifully*) Cruel as Mrs Coyle's remark was, it hit the target. Every morning I wonder to myself "Is this the day my soul soars like a dove leaving this old shell behind". (*Cheerfully again*) Not that I'd mind in the slightest. (*Quickly adding*) So long as it's after my first night. Then, in fact, if at the peak of my happiness as I stand there in the spotlights listening to the waves of applause, I could fall down plop on the boards I've trod so often, I'd be rapturously grateful.

Mrs Coyle claps her hands slowly

(*Acidly*) Thank you, Mrs Coyle.

Mrs Coyle Oh, I meant it. The finest example of hypocritical maudlin twaddle I've heard for many a year.

Everyone is speechless for a moment

Hattie I don't agree; I thought it was beautifully put.
Fay (*furious*) And it was not hypocritical. I meant every word.
Brigadier Yes, that was really below the belt, Mrs Coyle.
Mrs Coyle (*munching on*) I'm not a drama critic, or I might have added that it was overacted.
Fay How dare you! An old bag of rags—probably a lavatory attendant most of your life——
Bee Fay, dear——
Mrs Coyle If I had been—which I was not——
Fay Why? Did you fail the exam?
Mrs Coyle (*very pointedly*) I would still have considered it a more honourable way of earning a living than holding court in a stage dressing-room dressed only in a string of pearls.
Fay That was a hundred years ago. And was quite appallingly exaggerated. Anyway, how do you know? (*Realizing*) You've been snooping in my private papers.
Mrs Coyle If you leave your press-cutting books lying about——
Fay They've always been locked in my desk. Now I know what that broken-off knife blade I found was.
Mrs Coyle You're so old, you're addled. You lent them to me.
Fay That's an absolute lie.
Mrs Coyle (*to the others*) And I'll tell you something even more scandalous she did——
Bee (*firmly*) You will not, Mrs Coyle.
Mrs Coyle Not satisfied with a full-frontal exhibition——
Brigadier (*even firmer*) We do not wish to hear any more from you, Mrs Coyle.
Mrs Coyle Oh, you don't? (*Getting up without any sign of arthritis*) Then there's not much point in my staying is there.

She picks up Heloise's basket and stumps out

Hattie Oh dear, oh dear. I dreamt last night that something like this would happen; but nothing nearly so dreadful.
Brigadier She's taken that damn dog: that's what's dreadful.
Fay Oh, my darlings! I do apologize. I've never—well, hardly ever—said things like that. It must have been the unaccustomed sherry. I'm shattered and ashamed.
Bee We don't blame you: she was abominably rude.
Nan Rude or not, we've somehow got to get her back.
Hattie Yes, we simply must.
Brigadier (*to Fay*) You wouldn't—just because it's so important to us—consider apologizing and persuading her to return?
Fay No, I would not!
Bee Fay, you can afford to. You're a great star, and she's a mere nothing.

Act I, Scene 2 23

Nan It would show a wonderfully generous spirit.
Hattie You have so much; she has so little.
Brigadier Even she couldn't resist your charm if you lavished it.
Fay It's unfair. You'll make me feel ungrateful and vindictive if I don't.
Nan Then you will?
Fay I owe you so much that I shall have to. (*Going to the door*) Actually it might be quite fun acting the martyr.
Bee Bless you.
Hattie If all else fails attract her with the roast beef.

Fay goes out

Bee Now what?
Hattie We're in the most frightful muddle.
Brigadier None of that defeatist talk, Hatfield. We must make a quick reappraisal.
Nan (*looking towards the sofa*) At least we've got basket "B" in all right.
Hattie But not in the right place.
Bee Does that really matter?
Brigadier No. But how are we going to get "H" out with her sitting in the vehicle?
Nan We must stop her sitting in it; I'll take it out. (*She starts towards bedroom door with it*)
Brigadier No, no! We need it to take basket "H" out in.
Nan Damn; so we do.
Hattie How else can we stop her sitting in it?

They all ponder

Bee First we'd better stop them thinking we've just sat here plotting. (*She goes to the door and calls*) Mrs Honeywell; we're ready. (*She comes back and collects the plates*) My lovely mousse; all wasted. It took eight eggs, too.
Brigadier Damn your eggs. How are we going to switch?
Nan I think we've got to go back to the broken chair.
Hattie But it's not broken.
Nan (*thinking it out*) If it were, we could put it on one side so she couldn't sit in it. And then use it as planned.
Brigadier You mean break it.
Bee My lovely tub chair?
Brigadier We've all got to make sacrifices in this situation, Beatrice.
Hattie I'll mend it for you, Dame Beatrice.
Brigadier Can we break it, that's the point?
Nan We need something to bash it.
Brigadier What about the poker? (*He picks it up*)
Nan That should do.
Bee Not too much, please! Just one leg.
Brigadier I'm not a professional smasher, Beatrice. It'll have to take its chance. (*But as he lifts the poker ...*)
Nan Look out, I hear them.

Brigadier (*swinging the poker as they come in*) Play the shot like that, I said, and you'll get a birdie.

Fay and Mrs Coyle come in

Fay We agree we've been naughty, and'll behave like angels in the future. Don't we?
Mrs Coyle (*going to the tub and sitting in it*) You said you would. (*She puts Heloise's basket at her feet*)

Mrs Honeywell brings in a tray with the joint and vegetables

Mrs Honeywell You've been so long I thought the first course had poisoned you.
Bee You're just jealous because I made it.
Mrs Honeywell Who couldn't with so many eggs? Don't forget I want enough left over to make cottage-pie tomorrow.

She goes out, taking the mousse and plates

Bee I'm so sorry. She has a nip of gin now and then, and forgets we're not school-children. Carve away, Bertie.
Nan (*eyeing Heloise*) Yes, it'd be nice to get on with things. (*To Mrs Coyle*) I'm still worried about that chair: you'd be far safer in one of these.
Mrs Coyle Stop fussing. I hope there's Yorkshire pudding?
Bee And roast potatoes.
Mrs Coyle Good. Love roast potatoes. The more roasted the better.
Brigadier (*putting meat in front of her*) Will that do you, Fay?
Fay Far too much, monster. An eighth of that'd be overdoing it.
Brigadier Then I'll give that to you, Mrs Coyle.
Mrs Coyle (*looking at it with dissatisfaction*) Not at all too much for me.
Brigadier (*nodding significantly to Nan*) I have a good idea! Why don't I let you choose from the whole dish of potatoes.
Mrs Coyle Sensible.

She examines the potatoes Bee holds before her. During the following Nan, with her foot, scoops Heloise's basket towards her. When it's in reach she hastily dumps it on the sofa

Bee Then you can have exactly what you like.
Mrs Coyle Then that one. (*Searching*) That's the only really well-done one, isn't it?
Bee What about that one?
Mrs Coyle (*taking it*) Not bad. And I think probably—that.
Bee No, don't have that. I remember the shape when I peeled it—(*watching Nan out of the corner of her eye*)—and I nearly didn't include it as it didn't look very nice.
Mrs Coyle That one's a bit pale, but at least it's big.
Bee (*seeing Nan still struggling*) Surely you could manage one more?
Mrs Coyle Well, since you press me: that one. Hope there's gravy?
Bee Of course. And spinach.

Hattie serves these

Act I, Scene 2

Fay Spinach. How scrumptious. And so good for the complexion.

Nan is about to replace the false basket as Mrs Coyle turns and talks to her. She hastily puts it down, and stands screening it

Mrs Coyle Aren't you going to join us for the meal, Miss Parry?
Nan Oh, yes, I am, I am. (*Fiddling with it*) I was just having a little trouble with my suspender belt. So sorry.
Bee (*to Mrs Coyle*) You haven't got any horse-radish.
Mrs Coyle Don't like it.

Bee immediately spoons some on to her plate. As the ensuing scene goes on Nan turns to take up the basket, and realizes she doesn't know which is which

I said I didn't like it!
Bee Oh, I thought you said you did like it.
Mrs Coyle No, no, I don't. Look you've got it all over the best potato.
Bee (*doing so*) Well, I'll scrape it off, and then you'll never notice.
Mrs Coyle I shall.
Bee (*watching Nan*) Well, try. And then taste. And then we'll see.

Noticing Nan's dilemma, Bee gestures to her nose, and sniffs loudly. Mrs Coyle looks up at her

I'm sorry. I think the horse-radish has got up my nose a little.

Nan has understood the sign, and smells the baskets in turn. And triumphantly picks up the one which obviously smells

It is strong: you're right. I'm afraid all your potatoes will be a bit impregnated. I tell you what. (*Seizing up the potato dish*) Put yours back on that side, and then choose fresh ones.
Mrs Coyle (*choosing*) Not much of a choice left.

As she does this Nan gets the false basket back to near Mrs Coyle. Then stands wondering how to get the other out of the room. She notices the large embroidered shawl draped over the sofa, and takes it up

Nan Oh, disaster, disaster! The whole thing's disintegrating. It's the damn laundry. Oh, how shameful. (*Wrapping the shawl round herself and the basket, she hobbles towards the door*) I've never been so embarrassed. It's got all tangled up. You'll have to excuse me a moment.

She gets out with the basket hidden

Bee (*brightly*) She's always having trouble with her suspender belt.
Brigadier I'm surprised they're even worn nowadays.
Bee You'd have a few more surprises if you could see her underwear drawer. But what are you thinking of, Bertie? Where's the wine?
Brigadier Bless my soul, indeed what am I thinking about. (*Starting to go to the door*) I'll fetch it.
Fay No, no, we must have the champagne.

The Brigadier stops not knowing what to do

Bee I don't think champagne goes very well with beef.
Mrs Coyle Champagne goes well with anything. Open it up.
Fay Yes, open it, dear Brigadier: one of the most evocative sounds in the world.
Bee (*seizing the bottle*) I'll open it, then. Because I shall have claret. Get me a half-bottle, Bertie.
Brigadier Where do you think I'm going to get——(*Seeing her look*) Oh, yes, you mean one of those hidden-away ones. Won't be a sec ...

He hurries off

Bee (*taking the foil off the champagne bottle*) I'm so sorry: we're not usually so disorganized. Is the meat tender?
Fay Melts in the mouth.
Mrs Coyle I'll have rarer slices for my second helping. That's how Heloise likes it, too. (*Looking at the false basket*) Oh, the poor little poppet! Greedy forgetful old Mummy has forgotten her little pet. Wait a moment my angel. Mummy'll cut you up a bit very fine.

As she does this Bee and Hattie pause in horror

Bee Oh, I shouldn't give her any now.
Mrs Coyle (*cutting up*) Of course she must have her little Sunday treat.
Hattie I'm not at all sure that horse-radish isn't poison to dogs.
Mrs Coyle None got near the meat so it'll be all right. (*Getting up*) Now my poppet.

She starts to go towards the basket. Hattie seizes the potato dish and throws it on the floor. Consternation

Fay My dear child!
Mrs Coyle What on earth?
Hattie It slipped from my hands: I am sorry.
Bee It doesn't matter at all, dear. I never liked that old dish.
Mrs Coyle Awful waste of good potatoes.
Bee (*getting between Mrs Coyle and "Heloise"*) Mind where you're walking! I don't want them trodden into the carpet. Help me pick them up, will you?
Mrs Coyle (*helping collect potatoes*) The floor seems fairly clean. We'll still be able to eat them.

The Brigadier comes back with a bottle of claret

Hattie (*anxiously*) All right, Brigadier?
Brigadier Mission accomplished. I mean I've found the claret. But no halves, Beatrice, so I've opened a proper one.
Bee Pour it quickly: I need it.
Mrs Coyle What about the champagne?

Nan comes back. She has the shawl spread along one arm so that the other can't be seen. She sidles towards the sofa, tapping her heels, and singing an air from "Carmen"

Nan Tra, la, la, la la—lal la lal la la——

Act I, Scene 2   27

Fay (*clapping*) My darling, what a sublime entrance! But why?
Nan The shawl inspired me. I remembered Goya and Bizet and toreadors and—(*lamely*)—thought I'd be Spanish for a moment.
Fay You ridiculously whimsical creature. But come and eat your delicious beef before it gets stone cold.
Nan (*half-lying on the sofa*) I must just get back my breath.
Mrs Coyle (*having collected potatoes in her napkin*) And I'm getting back to the little beef I have left. Oh! I've forgotten Heloise's tit-bit.

As she's about to turn to the false basket . . .

Bee No!

Mrs Coyle turns to her

   No, Bertie, don't open the champagne till we're ready! Cover your ears everyone—(*doing so herself*) this one makes a frightful bang—could damage your ear-drums.
Fay (*covering her ears*) I must say it can make one jump out of one's skin.

As they cover their ears and watch the Brigadier, Nan slides the basket off the sofa and switches the two, hiding the false one on the sofa

Brigadier (*watching Nan*) All ready everyone?
Mrs Coyle (*impatiently*) Yes, yes, yes.
Brigadier (*counting slowly*) Then—one—two . . . (*Seeing Nan still not ready*) Wait a sec, wait a sec, I'll start again: one, two, three, and—bang. (*He eases out the cork; it makes no noise*) Oh. But what's a bang between (*nodding approvingly at Nan*) clever friends.
Mrs Coyle Now my poppet. (*She starts towards the basket with her plate*)
Nan (*swiftly removing it from her hand, and taking it to the Brigadier*) Refill, please Brigadier.
Brigadier Two bloody slices coming up.

Nan eases Mrs Coyle to her place, and sits herself

Nan Now, I'm sure you could manage another potato.
Brigadier (*handing Mrs Coyle her plate*) I've put those messy little bits in a napkin for you. Then you can take them and give them to her when you get back.
Mrs Coyle (*tucking in again*) Have to admit it's good beef.
Brigadier A little more for you, Fay?

A muffled bellow from Mrs Coyle

Hattie What is it, Mrs Coyle?

Mrs Coyle points to her closed mouth and speaks loudly, but incomprehensibly

Brigadier What's she say?

Mrs Coyle mumbles an even more urgent complaint. And stands up

Nan It seems to be something to do with her mouth.

Bee Of course it's her mouth with all that pointing. (*Very clearly, as if to a deaf person*) What is the matter with your mouth?
Mrs Coyle (*unintelligibly*) The potato.
Brigadier What's that?
Mrs Coyle (*shouting just as unintelligibly*) The potato!
Hattie I think she said "potato".
Brigadier Potato? She's gone potty.
Mrs Coyle (*furiously unintelligible*) No, potato, not potty. Potato. Your potato. Cracked my plate.
Nan Got it! It's her false teeth. The potato cracked her plate.
Bee Rubbish.
Mrs Coyle (*picking up her basket*) It's not rubbish! It's all in pieces. I shall sue.
Brigadier Can't get a word of it.
Hattie She's going to sue.
Bee You're right Bertie: she is potty.
Mrs Coyle Oh, no I am not! (*With her mouth only slightly open but the threat coming through clearly*) As you'll find when you hear from my solicitor. We'll sue. We'll sue the lot of you!

She marches out

Hattie Oh, how awful!
Fay If it's her false teeth it's her own fault. She's too mean to go to the dentist so uses glue to mend them.
Hattie But supposing she does sue?
Fay Lovely publicity. I'll perjure myself as much as you like.
Bee She won't sue. She chose the potato.
Nan Bet the old brute'll have a good try, though. Remember all those solicitors' letters about her fall over the carpet?
Brigadier She has no case whatsoever. Don't worry: we shan't hear another thing from her.

But at that moment there's a distant wail from Mrs Coyle

I seem to be wrong.
Fay With any luck she's swallowed the lot, glue and all.
Hattie No, that was a different sort of noise. (*With her fingers to her mouth*) I think she's found out.
Fay What?
Bee Hattie means she sounds as if she's found out— something else she didn't want to find out.

Another wail from Mrs Coyle

Nan She definitely has.
Fay But what?
Bee We think Heloise has gone ... (*She points upwards*)
Fay Thank goodness!
Brigadier (*feelingly*) The only pity is that Mrs Coyle didn't go with her.
Fay (*fervently*) Hear, hear.

Bee Yes. (*Thoughtfully*) We never thought of that, did we?
Nan (*slowly*) No, we didn't. But is there any reason we shouldn't think about it now?
Hattie What?
Brigadier No, by Jove! If we planned something along the same lines ...
Nan It would be easier in a way with a person.
Fay What are you talking about, my darlings?
Bee Nothing, dear, nothing! Just a rather brilliant little idea that struck us all at the same time. (*Brightly*) Do have some more champagne ...

CURTAIN

ACT II

Scene 1

The same. Ten days later. Afternoon

Hattie is standing on a chair having the hem of a very odd-looking dress pinned by Nan. Bee is sorting through a box of lace and ribbons

Hattie Mind! That pin nearly stuck into me!
Nan Sorry. Only one more. There. (*Standing back*) That any better?
Bee (*after a moment's examination*) No.
Hattie Oh, Dame Beatrice.
Bee I'm sorry, Hattie, but it isn't. This is evidently going to be quite a fashionable first-night. You don't want to look out of place.
Hattie (*miserably*) I shall anyhow, so does it matter?
Nan Does that mean you don't want to go?
Hattie It certainly does not! I shall go even if it has to be in my birthday suit.
Bee Keen as Fay is on publicity I think even she'd veto that. What about this beautiful ostrich feather?
Nan We're not dressing a chorus-girl for the *Folies Bergère*.

The Brigadier comes in

Brigadier I want to discuss——(*Breaking off on seeing Hattie*) What on earth are you doing up there in that get up?
Hattie (*climbing down*) Being made the butt of doubtful jokes. Which I don't appreciate.

She goes off

Brigadier Nerve-tonic run out again?
Bee She's worried about her first-night dress. I hope you're not wearing that rather more than green tail-coat.
Brigadier (*huffily*) No, it's shrunk. When I tried the damn thing on it split all over the place.
Nan So what are you going to do?
Brigadier Rely on Sergeant Waller: he'll find me something.
Bee Sergeant Waller? The man you've got upstairs decorating little Mrs Mackintosh's flat?
Brigadier Correct.
Nan How is a builder going to assure your sartorial elegance?
Brigadier He's really only the builder's mate. But being my ex-batman can

Act II, Scene 1

turn his hand to anything. Marvellous chap: the biggest wangler in the regiment. And darned my socks beautifully.

Nan So is he going to "run up" a dinner-jacket?

Brigadier No, no, no! But he keeps in touch with the chaps. One of them'll produce something.

Bee I may be pessimistic but I have an idea Fay will hide when she sees us four coming into the theatre.

Hattie comes back. She is dressed ordinarily again

Hattie (*quickly closing the door*) Psst!
Bee What?

Hattie mouths silently, pointing at the door

Brigadier What do you mean——? (*He repeats her gesture*)
Hattie Shh! (*Whispering*) You know who's at the door.
Brigadier I find it amazingly annoying when you go into your Soviet Spy act, Miss Hatfield.

Mrs Honeywell opens the door

Mrs Honeywell Sorry; but it'd have meant fisticuffs to keep her out.

Mrs Coyle pushes in. Mrs Honeywell goes out

Mrs Coyle I know I said I'd never come here again.
Bee You also said you weren't speaking to us.
Mrs Coyle I'm not speaking as a person. But as a tenant.
Nan You have a complaint?
Mrs Coyle I have. Those two old sisters in the flat have acquired a cat. I'm not prepared to put up with the noise it makes.
Hattie Siameses always talk.
Mrs Coyle It's not talk! It's yowling and screaming.
Hattie Only because you don't understand what it's saying.
Mrs Coyle (*furiously*) I understand when it scoops the chicken off the very plate in front of me.
Brigadier This is really getting us nowhere.
Mrs Coyle Then I will. Either they get rid of that cat, or I inform the management they're keeping it against the rules.
Hattie You wouldn't!
Nan After you had a pet yourself all those years?
Mrs Coyle But haven't now. And realize why the rule was made. Either it goes, or I report them.

She goes off

Brigadier Witch. I knew we should have gone on thinking about exterminating her.
Hattie We agreed we're here to help, not punish, Brigadier.
Brigadier (*grumbling*) You agreed; I didn't.

There's a tap on the door, and Dolores comes in. She has a new hair-style

Dolores Hi, everyone!
Bee Dolores, my dear. (*Gasping*) Oh, my goodness! Which of us has forgotten?
Dolores Panic not, panic not. It's only a quick pop-in. I'm doing a perm round the corner, so thought I'd bring this. (*She brings a cardboard box from under her arm*)
Bee If it's another present we shall refuse it.
Dolores No, no, just a loan. For Miss Hatfield.
Hattie Me?
Dolores But I shan't be a bit hurt if you say no. It's just that my friend's about the same size as you, so I thought it might do for the first night. (*She takes out a simple long dress*)
Nan Lovely colour. Let's see. (*She holds it up against Hattie*)
Bee Wonderful.
Hattie (*looking down at herself*) Yes, it really is, isn't it. Oh! (*She flings her arms round Dolores and kisses her, then backs away again*) Oh, I'm so sorry. I don't usually kiss people. It was the relief.
Dolores Don't worry, dear. I like being kissed.
Bee Does Bob oblige?
Dolores Oh, Bob's gone ages ago. I've got Chuck now.
Bee Oh, dear, I do wish you'd find a permanent one.
Dolores Well, you never know. Chuck's a great hulk with eye-lashes you could sweep the floor with. And his hair: sort of blue-black: all curls. I can't keep my fingers out of it. (*Putting the lid on the box*) I'll leave the box for when I collect the dress back. Will you still go even if?
Nan Even if what?
Dolores Oh, heck! You haven't heard?
Bee What?
Dolores (*awkwardly*) I thought they'd have told you so that you could sort of—see her through it, so to speak.
Brigadier For God's sake, girl: see who through what?
Dolores Fay Lombard.
Hattie Is she in some sort of trouble?
Dolores (*even more awkwardly*) I do the hair of the mum of a girl who works in the box office. Evidently they've been very worried about Fay. But it's not remembering the words that's done it.
Bee Done it? You mean they're going to sack her?
Dolores I'm afraid it seems like it.
Hattie (*crying out*) Oh, no!
Nan They couldn't!
Dolores They were having a meeting this afternoon to decide definitely.
Brigadier But they might not?
Dolores Elsie didn't hold out much hope. She said they'd interviewed two other old girls.
Hattie Oh, how dreadful!
Dolores I wish I hadn't told you.
Bee No. Thank you, dear. I'm glad you did.
Dolores If there's any way I can help you've only got to ask.

Act II, Scene 1

Bee Yes, we know.
Brigadier If you can find out for sure, will you ring?
Dolores She works in a shop so it's no good now, but I'll get on to Elsie's mum as soon as I get home tonight. And give you a bell.
Brigadier We shall be obliged.
Dolores Sorry to bring such bad news. But perhaps it won't be so bad after all.

She goes out

Hattie It's the most dreadful news I've ever heard in my whole life.
Nan Shattering.
Bee The poor old darling.
Brigadier Now, wait a sec, wait a sec. We don't know for certain it's true.
Nan I have a horrible idea it is. I went through her last scene with her yesterday, and she got the names more muddled than ever.
Hattie What are we going to do?
Brigadier Wait till she comes back from rehearsal, and then if she knows: pour alcohol into her, I suppose.
Nan And if she doesn't know?
Bee Do something before she does.
Nan What?

They all think

Brigadier Is there no way we can find out for certain?
Hattie We should have got Dolores to give us the mother's telephone number, then we could have rung and rung and caught her immediately she gets back.
Brigadier (*crossly*) Well, we didn't.
Nan (*picking up a newspaper*) But you're on the right lines, Hattie.
Hattie How?
Nan (*searching the paper*) Where are the damn theatres? They've left them out. No, here they are. Good. (*Reading*) Preview. Opening. Ah, here it is: box office.
Bee They won't tell you.
Nan (*dialling*) We can try. What appeals to box offices?
Brigadier Orders for hundreds of stalls, I should think.
Nan (*into the phone, speaking in a very old frail voice*) Box office? ... I wonder if you'd be so kind as to help me, dear? I live in Cornwall, just south of Truro——
Brigadier What on earth interest can that be to her?
Nan (*into the phone*) I want to come up and see a matinée of a play which I believe has an actress I used to be very fond of when I was a gal. But I'm nearly ninety, and it's a long way to go, and I do get a little confused. Is she in your play? (*She listens*) Fay Lombard. (*She listens*) Oh. (*She listens*) I see. (*She listens*) You're sure of that? (*She listens*) Thank you so much, dear. (*She puts down the phone*)
Hattie What, what?
Nan (*sadly*) It's not worth my making the journey.

Hattie No!
Nan She said she shouldn't tell me till it's announced tomorrow, but she'd just heard that Fay was "indisposed", and wouldn't be appearing.
Brigadier My God!
Bee How absolutely terrible.
Hattie It's worse. It's completely appalling.

They all pause in silent distress

Surely there's something we can do?
Nan If there is I can't think of it.
Bee It's not as if we knew anyone in the theatre we could—lean on.
Brigadier I can't think what it'll do to her.
Bee I'm afraid I can. She'll disintegrate completely.
Nan Yes; think what a poor old thing she was till she got this chance.
Hattie Oh, I feel quite terrible for her.
Bee She'll be so ashamed after all her excitement.
Brigadier And no salary.
Nan Probably terribly in debt: buying that coat and everything.
Hattie Oh, don't, don't: it's too ghastly to think about. Poor, poor Fay.
Nan She'll never be able to face it. It'll kill her.

A pause

Bee Yes, it probably will. (*Slowly, in a very low voice*) Unless we do it first.
Hattie (*horrified*) Dame Beatrice!
Brigadier What are you saying, Beatrice!
Bee (*thinking it out*) Do you remember when she told us she'd be glad to just—plop out?
Nan Yes, she did, didn't she.
Hattie But that was when she was buoyed up with the thought of success!
Bee Then surely even more vital if it stops her facing shame and misery.
Nan It's awful; but I think you're right.
Brigadier I certainly feel it's what she'd choose, if she had the choice.
Hattie But it'd be the most terrible thing to do!
Bee For us, yes. For her: I really believe an immense relief.
Hattie But we couldn't!
Brigadier We could. We have the means: if we have the courage.
Nan We must have it. We can't let her suffer as she will.
Hattie But she only said that about—fading away instantly, when she was going to be at the peak of her first-night happiness. This'd be in the depths of despair.
Nan (*thinking*) If they only decided this afternoon they're fairly certain not to have told her yet. We must act before she gets in that despair.
Hattie (*frantically*) But she still wouldn't be at the peak of happiness!
Bee Could we create a peak?
Brigadier How?
Bee (*impatiently*) I don't know how, Bertie! I just thought that if we could come up with something that'd give her enormous pleasure ...

Act II, Scene 1

Nan What does she like? Food to a certain extent. Flowers. Really nothing that's not connected with the theatre.
Bee She was over the moon about that little mention in the *Sunday Telegraph*. If we could somehow get her bigger publicity ...
Nan (*slowly*) Or the promise of bigger publicity. (*Excitedly*) Suppose we got someone here to interview her—tell her it was going to be in all the newspapers, with a large photograph ...
Brigadier I think you have it, Miss Parry! That'd immediately thrill her.
Nan Maybe even a TV appearance ...
Brigadier It's definitely the basis.
Hattie (*agitatedly*) But the basis of what? Think: it's a terrible, terrible, step ...
Brigadier (*kindly*) Do you want to see her exist in despair and enormous mental distress?
Hattie No, we can't let her do that. But surely——
Nan She's an actress through and through. She'll dramatize it, and feel the pain even more than an ordinary person.
Bee Knowing her love of glamour and excitement—how will she manage without it?
Hattie Yes, that's true. But we can't. We can't!
Bee (*quietly firm*) We can, Hattie. And must. We're always moaning about not being able to help anyone. Well, here's where we can. Instead of being feeble and afraid, we must do it.
Hattie (*trying to convince herself*) I know it would be best. But it's so terrible. Couldn't we just postpone it a bit?
Brigadier You know we can't. Once she knows it'll be too late.
Nan Yes, it's now or never.
Brigadier Then it's now. (*Briskly*) And we've no time to waste. Action, everyone.
Bee (*impatiently*) We've first got to decide on the action, Bertie.
Brigadier Oh, yes. (*Getting his clip-board*) I'll draw up the plan. What's first?
Nan To get her in here.
Brigadier No trouble. If we wave from the window when we see her returning, she'll pop in as she's often done. (*Writing*) Guard to be stationed at window.
Bee Then when she's here this reporter chap arrives.
Hattie But there isn't a reporter chap!
Brigadier We must find someone.
Nan What about that spotty godson of yours, Dame Beatrice? Isn't he an actor?
Bee (*shaking her head*) Failed. Now a waiter in Hammersmith.
Hattie In any case there's no time to contact anyone. We shall have to give it all up.
Brigadier We will not. Who else do we know?
Nan Of course it doesn't necessarily have to be a man.
Brigadier No. Dolores?
Bee I don't think she'd convince.

Brigadier Why not? She's only got to put on a different voice, and pretend ——(*He breaks off suddenly*) Different voice. Of course—it's you, Miss Parry.
Nan Me!
Bee Yes, you could probably get away with it.
Hattie But Fay knows Nan!
Brigadier Knows her as Nan. But speaking differently...
Nan Looking different: she's never seen me in a dress.
Bee And she's very short-sighted anyhow.
Nan I can wear a hat and spectacles.
Brigadier (*writing it down*) Reporter: Miss Parry. Now—how to administer.
Nan That's a bit more ticklish. Tea?
Bee No, she has a cup of tea in the theatre.
Nan Sherry, that's what she doesn't mind. Or what she really likes, of course, is champagne. (*Going to the sideboard*) This second bottle we never used at the party.
Brigadier (*working it out*) It'll be easiest if we have it already poured out. And—doctored. Where's the stuff?
Hattie Oh, do you think we must?
Nan (*fetching an ornament and unscrewing the false bottom*) Very good hiding-place you made, Hattie.
Brigadier (*writing it down*) Bottle. I'll do your roller trick, Miss Parry: best to have it powdered again, I think.
Hattie (*wide-eyed*) You're going to put it in the bottle of champagne?
Brigadier No, no. That's why it's got to be already poured out. Just one glass will be—the one.
Hattie (*panicking*) But that's terribly dangerous: someone else might get it.
Brigadier I'll mark it distinctly.
Hattie How?
Brigadier (*writing*) Orange. In THE one I'll put a slice of orange. They often do that.
Hattie Who do?
Brigadier (*heatedly*) It doesn't matter who does. I will. Is it quite clear: a slice of orange in THE one?
Nan Understood.

The others nod

Brigadier Now, what next?

As they all think Hattie lets out a horrified gasp

Bee What is it, Hattie?
Hattie Uum... (*She chews her lips in embarrassment*)
Brigadier Come on, come on: we may not have much time.

Hattie mumbles too low for them to hear

  What's she mumbling about?
Nan Tell me, dear.

Act II, Scene 1

Hattie whispers in Nan's ear

Oh, yes. She's worried about—about, er, the ...
Brigadier Now for God's sake don't you start.
Nan She's worried about—the mortal remains.
Brigadier My God, yes, the corpse.
Hattie Oh, please don't call it that, Brigadier!
Brigadier Whatever we call it, we've got to do something with it. What?

They all ponder

Bee I really don't think there's anything we can do.
Hattie (*hopefully*) That means we'll have to call the whole thing off.
Brigadier It doesn't mean anything of the sort. Nan?
Nan I'm afraid this time I'm foxed. (*Thinking*) We've got to get it—taken away, somehow.
Brigadier (*stroking his chin and looking down*) Yes, but it's not exactly the sort of thing one can smuggle out. (*Suddenly*) My socks!
Nan What?
Brigadier My socks. Sergeant Waller who darned my socks: he's the chap.
Hattie The builder's mate?
Brigadier Yes, he could do it. (*Thinking it out*) Builders always have trenches, and concrete, and that sort of stuff. He'll wangle it. Wonder if they've left the building yet? Get him on the phone, Parry.
Nan (*rushing to the phone*) Mrs Mackintosh: I've got her number here somewhere.
Brigadier If she answers, don't let on it's us.

Nan dials the number

If it's Sergeant Waller, just say you've someone with an important message.
Nan (*hissing*) It's Mrs Mackintosh. (*Into the phone, speaking in a cockney accent*) 'Ullo? Is that Mrs Mackintosh's flat? ... Oh, ta. Sorry if you're in the middle of your tea-break, luv, but I want to 'ave a word with the chap what's painting. ... Er ... (*Frantically, in a whisper to the Brigadier*) Norman or Bert?
Brigadier Haven't the foggiest.
Nan (*desperately*) You must say.
Brigadier He looked most like a Norman.
Nan (*into the phone*) Sorry the 'old up, Mrs Mac. Dropped me fag. It's Norman I want. (*To Brigadier*) She's calling him. (*Into the phone*) It's his mother. (*She passes the phone to the Brigadier*)
Brigadier As if I'll sound like his mother. (*Into the phone*) Is that Sergeant Waller? ... Good. Brigadier Appleby here. Urgent business. N.T.B.S.A. (*Shouting*) N.T.B.S.A. you fool! ... Good. Your van there? (*He listens*) Good. Your mate there? ... Good. Rendezvous here, at my flat, forthwith. Understood? Good. And don't forget: N.T.B.S.A. (*He puts down the phone*)
Hattie What's N.B.T. whatever it is?

Brigadier "Not to be Spoken About."
Bee Ah, yes.
Brigadier Good. Everything's shaping. (*Looking at his watch*) Seventeen hundred hours.
Bee That's about the time she usually comes back.
Brigadier Then "action" everyone.

No-one moves

Come along, come along, come along.
Hattie You must make it clear what we do, when.
Brigadier Thought it was. (*Looking at orders*) Guard at window. Yes, that's urgent. Hatfield!
Hattie Oh, must I?
Brigadier Yes. Other troops occupied other fronts.
Hattie (*going to the window*) What do I do?
Brigadier When you see her wave welcomingly.
Hattie I shall feel such a traitor.
Brigadier Parry, you go and tog up.
Nan (*going to the door*) I must come in at just the right moment. How am I to know?
Brigadier Uum . . . ?
Bee I'll put on the gramophone.
Nan OK. As soon as I hear music I'll enter. N.T.B.S.A.

She goes out

Brigadier (*fetching the bottle of champagne*) Champagne. I'd better go and prepare.

He goes out

Bee (*calling after him*) Bertie!

The Brigadier re-appears

Brigadier What is it?
Bee You've forgotten the—method. (*She holds out the ornament*)
Brigadier Oh. (*Annoyed at his mistake*) I hadn't forgotten it actually. (*Snatching it*) I was doing things—in their proper military order.

He goes out

Bee It'd be so much easier if we could only do everything in a sensible civilian way.
Hattie The only way I want to do it is not at all. Oh, I feel awful. As if it's some terrible dream.
Bee (*going round tidying the room*) That's a good way to think of it, dear. A dream in which we're doing something we all hate, but which is kind and quick and merciful. I was thinking during the planning I wouldn't mind in the slightest if someone did it to me.
Hattie Oh, neither would I.

Act II, Scene 1

Bee Far better out like a candle than all the indignity and nastiness that might happen.
Hattie (*going to her*) Oh, yes, you're quite right when one thinks of it that way. You're a great comfort, Dame Beatrice.
Bee Good. But hadn't you better get back to your post?
Hattie (*scampering back to the window*) Oh, sorry. But even so we won't do it if she already knows, will we?
Bee No, I should feel differently then.
Hattie Oh, good, then there's still hope.

Mrs Honeywell comes in

Mrs Honeywell Two odd-looking men to see the Brigadier.
Bee Oh. Oh, yes: you'd better show them into his room.
Mrs Honeywell Into his room?
Bee Yes. He's—thinking of having it redecorated.
Mrs Honeywell I see. Wondered why they came with paint all over them.

She goes out

Hattie What about her?
Bee What about her?
Hattie Well, if she sees what's going on—if it goes on——
Bee Oh, my heavens, yes! We didn't think of that. We must get her out of the way.
Hattie Send her to get milk?
Bee The fridge's packed with milk. (*Looking round and seeing her desk*) An urgent note: that's it. (*She hurries to the desk*)
Hattie Who to?
Bee Anyone. Who's a bit far away? Veronica.
Hattie But you haven't time!
Bee (*taking an envelope and starting to address it*) Just an envelope. Call her.

Hattie flies to the door and calls

Hattie Mrs Honeywell! Just a moment, if you will. (*Coming back and speaking in a whisper*) But what excuse?
Bee (*licking up the envelope*) Haven't the remotest.

Mrs Honeywell comes back

Oh, Mrs Honeywell dear, will you be an angel and pop round with this urgent note to Mrs Lambert? Her telephone's out of order.
Mrs Honeywell (*taking the envelope*) Of course, Dame dear. I'll give it to the porter: he goes home that way.
Bee No! I mean—I particularly want you to give it to her. You see—she's stopped coming to see us, so we think—she's going to have a baby. Will you look?
Mrs Honeywell What fun. Right you are ... (*She starts to go*)
Bee Oh, wait a moment! We're just about to have a little celebration. And I'd rather like you to bring in the champagne the Brigadier's getting ready. Could you do that when I ring, and go immediately afterwards?

Mrs Honeywell I thought it was urgent?
Bee It is. But not five-minutes-less urgent.
Mrs Honeywell OK.

She goes off

Hattie Won't Veronica find it odd that you send her an urgent empty envelope?
Bee Yes. We'll think why when we've time.

The Brigadier comes in agitatedly

Brigadier No oranges!
Bee What?
Brigadier The slice of orange. There's nothing to slice.
Hattie What about a lemon?
Brigadier None of them either. Only an old banana.
Bee We can't serve champagne with rotting banana floating about in it. Mark the glass another way.
Hattie Put a pencil mark.
Brigadier (*angrily*) A pencil doesn't mark on glass.
Hattie (*panicking*) I'm sure someone's going to get the wrong glass. I'm sure!
Brigadier Quiet, woman.
Bee Could we chip one glass?
Brigadier No—I have it! I'll only half-fill the other glasses, and fully fill THE one. Understood?
Bee Much better: quite clear.
Brigadier (*starting to hurry out*) Must inform Parry.
Hattie (*frantically*) No, come back, Brigadier, come back!
Brigadier What is it?
Hattie I think it's Fay getting out of a taxi.
Brigadier Rubbish; she never takes taxis.

He hurries out

Bee (*hurrying to the window*) Why did you think it was her?
Hattie Well, it's very like her. Wait a moment—you can't see—she's dropped her bag.
Bee Where are Bertie's bird-watching glasses? (*She pick up binoculars*)
Hattie (*pointing*) There.
Bee (*watching through the glasses*) Yes, it's her all right. Odd her taking a taxi.
Hattie It must mean she's heard. Oh, thank goodness, thank goodness.
Bee I don't think you're right. She's happily waving to the man as he drives off. She's looking up. (*Waving*) Hullo. Hullo! She doesn't seem to see us.

Hattie flies to get the shawl, and waves it in front of the window

Ah, now she has. Waving back.

(*Coming away from the window*) She's gone in, and will now be on her way

Act II, Scene 1

up. I think I'd better make sure she doesn't by-pass us. (*Taking up the house phone*) Quick! Warn Nan.

Hattie flies out

(*Into the phone*) Oh, Porter. Dame Beatrice. Mrs Lombard's just come in, I think. As you put her in the lift will you tell her I'm expecting her? Thank you. (*She puts down the phone as . . .*)

Hattie flies in

Hattie Nan's ready.
Bee Did you warn Bertie, too?
Hattie You didn't tell me him.

She flies out again

Bee (*calling*) As Nan won't, he must be here when she arrives.

The house telephone rings. She answers it

Yes? (*She listens*) Oh, no! Tell her we don't mind how dishevelled she is. Persuade her: it's urgent. (*She puts down the phone as . . .*)

Hattie flies back

Hattie Brigadier just coming.
Bee Did you tell Mrs Honeywell to let her in?
Hattie No!

She rushes out again, bumping into the Brigadier as he hurries in

Sorry!
Brigadier A splendid scheme planned with Sergeant Waller.
Bee Good. How's he going to know when we want him? Have you given him a signal?
Brigadier Oh, my God . . .

He hurries out just missing Hattie as she returns

Hattie Mrs Honeywell alerted.
Bee Splendid. Anything else? Oh, the music. (*She rushes and puts a record on the old-fashioned machine*)

Hattie stands with her eyes closed

What's the matter; are you feeling faint?
Hattie No, just praying.

The Brigadier hurries back

Brigadier Told him we'd ring the hand-bell.
Bee (*agitatedly*) No, no, the hand-bell's the signal for Mrs Honeywell and the champagne!
Brigadier Dear God . . .

He rushes out again

Hattie He's going a bit scarlet in the face: hope he's not going to have a heart-attack.
Bee That's all we need.
Hattie (*going to the table*) Mine's knocking as if it's trying to get out. I think I'd better have some tonic.

The Brigadier comes back gasping

Brigadier If anything else needs doing, somebody else must do it. (*He sinks into a chair*)
Bee I've got my smelling-salts somewhere.
Hattie Would you like a little nerve-tonic?
Brigadier (*crossly*) Stop fussing around, and sit down. We must appear as if it's an ordinary evening. (*He opens a newspaper*)
Hattie (*fervently*) If only it were.

Mrs Honeywell comes in

Mrs Honeywell Mrs Lombard.

Mrs Honeywell goes out. Fay comes in

Fay My darlings. How typically sweet of you to ask me. Just exactly what I needed.
Hattie (*anxiously*) You've heard then?
Fay Heard what, my little one?
Bee (*hastily*) You heard from the porter we hoped you'd come?
Fay The most welcome invitation I could possibly have had. Though I would have liked to change first. I feel like a chewed rag. And am sure must look like one.
Bee (*anxiously*) Did today's rehearsal go badly then?
Fay Oh, no, darling. My scenes were wonderful. Everybody was so dear and sweet about them: I was really quite embarrassed. I'm still having a little trouble with those damn names, Nan—oh! Isn't she here?
Bee She went out. To—play bridge.
Fay Oh, I thought she told me she didn't play bridge.
Bee That's why she's gone out—to learn to play. Bridge lessons.
Fay How sensible. Everyone who's getting—near the wrong columns of *The Times* should learn bridge. The rows keep one on one's toes.
Hattie (*hesitatingly*) So the play—will open as planned?
Fay Of course, my little treasure. So long as I last out.

They all look at each other

I have to admit I do find rehearsals very fatiguing.
Bee That's what we thought. And why we're going to give you a little treat: champagne.
Fay Oh, you mustn't!
Brigadier It's one of the ones you brought.
Fay Then you must! What a divine thought: you really are too good to me.
Bee We'll give it a moment or two longer to get cold. Bertie forgot to put it in the fridge.

Act II, Scene 1

Fay You're forgiven, darling man. Because you're still the best-looking soldier I've ever known. And that is saying something.
Bee Shall we have a little music while we wait? I always find it very soothing when I'm tired. Put it on, Hattie, will you?

Hattie goes and starts the record

Fay (*doing so*) I shall lie back and let sublime sound wash over me and heal my tattered nerves.

They all relax. The music starts. It's the Funeral March. Bee suddenly realizes, and jumping up, rushes to turn the record over

Bee Oh! That side's got terrible scratches. Let's have the other.

As the other side starts Mrs Honeywell comes in

Mrs Honeywell Mrs Eleanor J. Wannamaker Junior.

Nan comes in practically unrecognizable. She is smartly dressed, with hat and glasses, and an American accent

Bee turns off the music

Mrs Honeywell exits

Nan Hi-ya, folks. Sorry to disturb such a peaceful domestic scenario, sweeties.
Bee Who are you?
Nan But that cutey little porter told me I'd find her here, so I said "Eleanor, never you mind if they think you're one of those pushy Americans, you go in and see her, gal."
Brigadier See who?
Nan (*approaching Fay*) This great Dame of the Stage that I've admired since I was knee-high to a grass-hopper. And my old Poppa before that. Said she was the most exciting and lovely baby he'd ever seen.
Fay (*delighted*) Oh, my darling!
Nan Said your modern film-stars were trash compared with her fresh and startling real beauty.
Brigadier I'm sure he was right.
Fay Oh, you are all too sweet.
Nan Said he actually had to fight to get a peep of her through the crowds of fans waiting at the stage door.
Fay It's true! And the flowers they threw. And sent. My dressing-room was often so full that I'd feel quite faint from the perfume.
Hattie Oh, how lovely.
Fay It was. (*To Nan*) And lovely of you, sweet creature, to remind me of such joyous days.
Nan But why I've come is to beg—yes, on my knees—(*she gets on them*)—a gigantic favour.
Fay No need to kneel, silly creature. Of course, what is it?
Nan You wouldn't have heard of Eleanor J. Wannamaker of course. But I'm quite a name on TV back in the States. So they've given me a little

programme here. Would you—I daren't hope—but I must ask: would you appear and be interviewed?
Fay (*breathlessly*) Appear on the television?
Nan I'll get one of those Sirs—one of those old stage knights—to be the interviewer. Don't say "no".
Fay I'm almost incapable of saying anything. But it would be the most exciting and exhilarating thing that's ever happened to me. Of course I agree.
Bee How thrilling. We really have something to celebrate now. (*She rings the hand-bell*)
Fay But clothes, my darling! I've nothing suitable for such an occasion.
Nan Have no worry, honey. We'll go off to that Bond Street of yours. You choose what you like. We foot the bill.
Fay My cup is full.

Mrs Honeywell comes in with a tray of glasses. Only one is fully filled. Mrs Honeywell goes out

Nan I've got my photographer in the lobby. I'd like to get a few nice pics for the tabloids. Can we rehearse one or two poses?
Fay Anything, darling. I feel so thrilled I could float for you if you wanted.
Nan I think one of your dazzling smiles—say, in that doorway—as if you were making an entrance?
Fay (*going and posing in the open bedroom doorway*) Just like old times.
Bee Perhaps with a glass of champagne in your hand?
Nan Brill.

Bee gives Fay the filled glass

Now: as if you were drinking to us . . .
Fay I am, my darlings, I am. To the sweetest and loveliest people in all the world who are giving me the most wonderful evening of my life.

She lifts the glass to her lips. And immediately falls out of sight into the bedroom, where there is the sound of falling and the crash of glass

The four stand motionless in horror. The Brigadier recovers first

Brigadier Come along, come along. No time for dithering. (*Hurrying to the door and calling*) Sergeant Waller!

Sergeant Waller and another elderly man in stained overalls appear at the door and stand to attention

Sergeant Sir!
Brigadier Action!

The two men hurry into the bedroom

(*Calling after them*) And make it snappy!
Bee We have the comfort that it was quite instant.
Hattie (*trying to assure herself*) And she was wonderfully, wonderfully, happy.

Act II, Scene 1   45

Nan There couldn't have been more of a peak of happiness.
Brigadier No, you did jolly well, Parry.
Bee I can't tell you what I felt like giving her the glass.
Brigadier Then don't. And don't think about it. Shh! I hear them coming. (*Looking at his watch*) Excellent time. Good men, good men . . .

The two men come out of the bedroom carrying a long rolled-up carpet. They stagger through the room with it and out of the front door

Hattie Was that—I mean—was that—was that . . .
Brigadier Quick Parry, they'll be in the hall in a jiffy. Get on to the porter.
Nan Get on to the porter? You never said anything about that in the planning.
Brigadier Don't do a Hatfield. Go on—improvise. He mustn't see the carpet.
Nan (*picking up the house phone*) Porter? He's not there!
Bee He must be there: he was when she came in.
Nan Oh, yes he is. (*Into the phone speaking in a Scots accent*) Oh, Porter? This is Mrs Mackintosh from the fourth floor . . .
Brigadier (*watching through his field-glasses, and commentating as if at a race-course*) They're coming out now . . .
Nan (*into the phone*) I've had a wee accident with my washing-machine . . .
Brigadier Going towards the van—faster, you fools, faster . . .
Nan (*into the phone*) No, not the dishes one the one I do my whites in . . .
Brigadier Opening rear doors. My God! There's a policeman.
Hattie
Bee } (*together; rushing to the window*) Oh, no!
Nan It may be because I'm using the wrong washing powder . . .
Brigadier Police approaching van. Police level with van.
Nan (*into the phone*) It's so confusing with so many on the television . . .
Brigadier Police past van.
Nan (*on the phone*) Well, it's not really so very bad . . .
Brigadier Carpet put in. Door being closed. Door stuck! Reopened. Slammed. Closed this time. Men hurrying to front of van.
Nan Just an inch of water all over the kitchen floor . . .
Brigadier Men in van. Doors being slammed. They're away!

Hattie and Bee sink into chairs

Nan (*into the phone*) But it's suddenly sinking fairly fast. I think I can cope. Thanks. (*She puts down the phone and sinks into a chair*)
Bee I've never, ever, felt so dreadful.
Hattie I'm numb.
Nan I don't approve of daytime rests, but I think I'll have to go and lie down.
Brigadier (*handing round champagne*) At least we may as well not waste this.
Hattie (*getting up*) Oh, not for me. I think I'll have some nerve-tonic though.

The others take glasses

Bee (*holding up her glass sadly*) To a very sad, but actually very successful operation.

Except for Hattie, they lift their glasses to their lips. And immediately fall back motionless. Hattie looks at them

Mrs Honeywell comes in

Mrs Honeywell I'm just off. Is there any message or just——(*She stops as she sees the bodies*) What's this?
Hattie I don't know! A silly joke. A very very silly joke. (*Going to Nan*) Now stop pretending—come on. (*In complete bewilderment*) Something's happened to them.
Mrs Honeywell What could have?
Hattie I don't know. (*Suddenly realizing*) You didn't do anything to the champagne, did you?
Mrs Honeywell Only sprinkled the glasses with the icing-sugar the Brigadier left.

Hattie sinks slowly back into a chair. There is the distant sound of bagpipes. Then voices:

Brigadier's voice Miss Hatfield!
Nan's voice Hattie!
Bee's voice Hattie, dear.
Hattie (*sitting up slowly, and looking up to the ceiling*) Yes?

Mrs Honeywell who obviously can't hear anything, looks at her in amazement

Brigadier's voice You're not to worry.
Nan's voice You're to keep quite calm.
Bee's voice And not be distressed at all.
Hattie Why?
Brigadier's voice We're going to return.
Nan's voice So try to wait patiently.
Bee's voice Because we shall come back to support and help you as soon as we can.

As Hattie gazes upwards——

—*the* CURTAIN *falls*

SCENE 2

The same, some weeks later

Mrs Coyle is sitting at the table enjoying the large tea laid out. She is listening to a banal piece of music on the record-player. She beats time with the teapot as she pours out another cup, and then delightedly sinks her teeth into the last piece of toast. She picks up the hand-bell, and rings it. She "conducts" the

Act II, Scene 2

music with her cup while she waits to drink from it. Then again, crossly, rings the bell

Mrs Honeywell comes in

Mrs Honeywell Yes?
Mrs Coyle Why didn't you come quicker?
Mrs Honeywell Because I haven't got a gold medal for running.
Mrs Coyle My, my, we are witty these days. I'll have some more buttered toast.
Mrs Honeywell I've already brought you a second lot.
Mrs Coyle Well, it's one thing you don't do too badly.
Mrs Honeywell (*acidly*) Thanks. (*She starts to go to the door*)

The music comes to an end

Mrs Coyle And I'll have some of that quince jam.
Mrs Honeywell That quince jam was brought as a special treat for Miss Hatfield.
Mrs Coyle Then it'll be ready here when she comes, won't it? If she comes. She's very late; where is she?
Mrs Honeywell At the police station.
Mrs Coyle Why? Don't say their great brilliance has found a clue at last?
Mrs Honeywell (*ironically*) They asked her—if she was passing—to collect her umbrella they'd taken by mistake.
Mrs Coyle You amaze me. Those blundering incompetent idiots made a mistake! (*Scornfully*) What's the whole enquiry been but one vast mistake from the very beginning. I could have done better myself.
Mrs Honeywell You should try.
Mrs Coyle I probably shall! But if she wasn't responsible for the deaths, why did our (*sneering*) beautiful Fay disappear?
Mrs Honeywell I imagine that's what they're still trying to find out.
Mrs Coyle Of course she did it. And more's the pity they won't be able to string her up when they find her.
Mrs Honeywell (*acidly*) I can think of a greater pity.

She goes out

Mrs Coyle looks towards the record-player, and starts to go to it. Then proceeds to search the room, poking into drawers, books etc. She hears something, darts back to the table, and is drinking tea when ...

Hattie comes in. She is dressed in bright colours

Hattie Sorry I'm a little late.
Mrs Coyle Thought the police must have found out something and locked you in a cell.
Hattie No, they gave me a cup of tea. But I wouldn't mind a rather weaker one if you'll be so kind.
Mrs Coyle (*feeling the pot*) It's only tepid now. I'll ring for more.
Hattie No, please. I don't want to bother her: she's so good.

Mrs Coyle (*acidly*) That's what you think. (*Shrugging*) But it's your flat now. It must be lovely to be a woman of property.
Hattie There's very little money: I don't see how I'm going to keep it up.
Mrs Coyle (*looking round*) You can always sell things.
Hattie (*strongly*) I wouldn't dream of it! I want everything left exactly as it is.
Mrs Coyle Why?
Hattie (*hesitatingly*) I have this strange feeling that they're all still here.
Mrs Coyle You'd better be careful or you'll go round the bend.
Hattie I'm not sure I'm not already round it a bit. This feeling's so strong. (*Looking up*) And I—hear things.
Mrs Coyle Those dreadful children upstairs. The parents have as much idea of training them as I would a herd of elephants.
Hattie No, not that sort of noise. Not that at all.
Mrs Coyle What then?
Hattie It always starts with—it seems ridiculous—but it always starts with—something that sounds like bagpipes.
Mrs Coyle You're not secretly drinking, are you?
Hattie I do have a thimbleful of sherry after I've heard them. Because it's a bit—unnerving. Not nastily unnerving: it's really rather nice.
Mrs Coyle (*scornfully*) What happens after these bagpipes?
Hattie Nothing happens. I just have the feeling that—well, sort of as if people are trying to telephone me.
Mrs Coyle You must be bilious. You'd better take a strong dose of something.
Hattie No. Because in a way I enjoy it. It's a comfort. That's why I've been able to get through these last awful weeks. It just worries me that I can't answer the telephone calls.
Mrs Coyle It's worse than biliousness. You'd better see the doctor. (*Anxiously*) Have you made your will?
Hattie No.
Mrs Coyle You'd better. I'll help you.

Mrs Honeywell comes in with the toast and jam which she puts on the table

Mrs Honeywell Oh, you're back, Miss Hattie dear. I'll make you a fresh pot.
Hattie No, don't worry. I really——
Mrs Coyle (*interrupting*) This isn't the quince!
Mrs Honeywell Isn't it?
Mrs Coyle You know perfectly well it isn't. This is shop strawberry. The muck you put in those soggy tarts.
Hattie I like those little tarts.
Mrs Honeywell Thank you, Miss Hattie dear.
Mrs Coyle Because you know nothing about cooking. If you did you'd see how the standard has steadily declined since the so-called "accident".
Mrs Honeywell (*suddenly flaring*) The quantity eaten certainly hasn't!

She flounces out

Act II, Scene 2

Mrs Coyle Obviously drunk again. Are you going to allow her to be rude to me like that?
Hattie (*slowly*) Yes. I think I am.
Mrs Coyle (*furious*) Typical. Typical of the feeble attitude that's let her get into her slack ways. If you take my advice, you'll sack her.

Hattie gets up, and slowly goes to the table on which are her glass and nerve-tonic

Did you hear what I said?
Hattie (*calmly*) Yes.
Mrs Coyle So are you going to do it?
Hattie (*equally calmly*) No.
Mrs Coyle You're very silly. She'll have you right under her thumb, and be giving you orders before you know where you are.

Hattie is pouring out a large tonic

You're not paying attention to what I'm saying.
Hattie No. (*She swallows most of the tonic*)
Mrs Coyle Why? (*Nastily*) Hearing bagpipes?
Hattie No.
Mrs Coyle Then why are you standing there like a ninny?
Hattie Waiting for my nerve-tonic to work.
Mrs Coyle If we're waiting for it to give you a little sense we're wasting our time. (*Going to the door*) I'm going to lie down until dinner.
Hattie (*for her, surprisingly firmly*) No, wait!
Mrs Coyle What?
Hattie Sit down; I want to say something.
Mrs Coyle This is going to be good! (*Sitting*) I'm all attention.
Hattie (*in even tones*) You moved in here because you persuaded me that your room next door needed re-decorating.
Mrs Coyle It did. It was damp, dark, and dirty.
Hattie You chose the awful colour that made it dark. You made it dirty. And Sergeant Waller told me there was no sign of damp.
Mrs Coyle That man and his barrack-room language.
Hattie Whatever he was driven to saying to you he made a very good job of the painting. It's been finished five weeks. Since then, I've suggested you go back several times. I've asked you to go back several times. Now, I order you—once—to go. Tomorrow. Or tonight, if possible. (*She sits down*)
Mrs Coyle (*nastily*) And if I refuse? As I have every intention of refusing.
Hattie I shall get the police. I have a lot of friends there now, and know they'll help me.
Mrs Coyle (*after a moment*) You could prove no misdemeanour; you've accepted my rent: you have no case whatsoever. I like this flat better than the other, and I shall remain here just—as—long—as—I—like.
Hattie (*suddenly crumbling*) Oh, no! (*In tears*) I can't bear it. I don't know what to do.

There is the faint sound of bagpipes. Hattie forgets her tears, slowly sits bolt upright, and looks upwards

Mrs Coyle Now what is it?
Hattie Don't you hear anything?
Mrs Coyle Of course I don't, because there's nothing to hear.

The music gets louder

Hattie You must hear it now.
Mrs Coyle For crying out loud. You're not at the Edinburgh Tattoo again?

Voices are heard calling

Brigadier's voice Miss Hatfield!
Nan's voice Hattie!
Bee's voice Hattie, dear.
Hattie (*faintly*) Yes?
Mrs Coyle What d'you mean "yes". You are hearing the bagpipes?
Brigadier's voice Tell the old brute to mind her own business.
Hattie (*to Mrs Coyle*) Mind your own business.
Mrs Coyle I beg your pardon!
Bee's voice Listen carefully to what we're going to say.
Hattie (*faintly*) All right.
Mrs Coyle What's all right?
Nan's voice Tell her to shut up.
Hattie (*to Mrs Coyle*) Shut up.
Mrs Coyle You tell me to shut up?
Hattie (*crossly to her*) Yes, I can't hear if you will keep talking.
Mrs Coyle (*getting up and going to the tea-table*) I think you'd better have a cup of cold tea.
Bee's voice Hattie dear, you're not to be frightened.
Hattie I'm not.
Mrs Coyle You're not what?
Nan's voice We're coming back to help you as we promised.
Hattie Oh, good!
Mrs Coyle Good you want a cup of tea, you mean?
Brigadier's voice It'll be a bit of a shock, but you're not to panic.
Hattie I won't; I'm looking forward to it.
Mrs Coyle (*looking at her in amazement*) What—cold tea?
Brigadier's voice Tell the old bag to leave you alone.
Hattie (*to Mrs Coyle*) You're an old bag, and you're to leave me alone.

Mrs Coyle drops the cup and saucer

Bee's voice You're quite sure you won't be frightened?
Hattie No, I shan't, I promise I shan't.
Mrs Coyle Have you gone crazy?
Nan's voice You're quite ready?
Hattie Yes.
Brigadier's voice Then: on parade troops.

Act II, Scene 2

The bagpipes blare out and the Brigadier, Bee, and Nan appear in different parts of the room. They are dressed almost as before; but somehow look ethereal

Hattie Oh! Hullo!
Mrs Coyle Hullo? But I've been here all the time.
Bee You can see us all right then, dear?
Hattie (*looking round at them*) Yes, I can. Quite clearly.
Nan Good. But you won't be able to hear us if those damn bagpipes go on.
Bee He arrived at the same time as us, and will insist on following us around. (*Calling up*) Thank you very much, Angus. That's lovely. But we have a little business to do. Could you go and play for someone else in the meantime?

There is a toot on the bagpipes, and they stop

Hattie Oh, it is lovely to see you!
Mrs Coyle After all those insults it's lovely to see me?
Hattie I'm absolutely delighted.
Nan So are we, Hattie dear.
Hattie Why didn't you come before?
Mrs Coyle (*going over and sniffing the tonic bottle*) That can't be nerve-tonic you've been taking.
Bee Well, it's very difficult, dear.
Brigadier All a bit N.T.B.S.A.
Bee As we're new at it we're not absolutely sure how it works.
Hattie But you're happy?
Mrs Coyle No, I am not!
Nan Oh, yes, it's glorious.
Brigadier Very well organized. It may become a bit monotonous if it goes on for ever . . . (*Adding quickly, looking up*) Not that I'm complaining!
Nan Now we have a lot to do . . .
Bee As this is our first time, we may not be allowed long . . .
Brigadier So we must quickly get rid of that appalling woman.
Hattie I can't. I've tried!
Mrs Coyle (*who has been watching her*) You've been taking drugs all this time. I shall have this bottle analysed.
Bee As it's such a bad case we've got dispensation to help you.
Hattie Oh, good!
Mrs Coyle You don't mind it being analysed?
Hattie But I don't know how you can possibly succeed.
Mrs Coyle I'll succeed all right. And if it proves to be drugs you'll be in gaol, my girl.
Brigadier Don't worry: five minutes, and she'll be out.
Hattie Oh, that would be good.
Mrs Coyle You are potty: no-one could want to go to jail.
Hattie Can't she see you at all?
Nan Nor hear us. So it's pretty easy. Start by telling her the flat's haunted.
Mrs Coyle Are you hearing those voices again?

Hattie (*to her*) Yes. They say the flat's haunted.
Mrs Coyle Fiddlesticks! By what?
Hattie (*to the others*) By what?
Mrs Coyle That's what I said, by what.
Brigadier Ghosts, of course. No need to stick too clearly to facts. Make it scary. Use your imagination.
Hattie You know I'm not good at thinking things up.
Mrs Coyle I'm not asking you to think it up. I'm asking what these marvellous voices are saying, little Miss Joan of Arc?
Bee Tell her it's not only voices.
Hattie (*to Mrs Coyle*) It's not only voices.
Mrs Coyle (*sarcastically*) No, it's bagpipes, too, I know.
Nan And shapes.
Bee Strange shapes moving about all the time.
Hattie There are strange shapes moving about all over the place. Floating. And weaving. And coming and going.
Brigadier Fine! Pile it on.
Hattie (*pitifully*) I'm at the bottom of the pile: I can't think of any more.
Mrs Coyle Ah, ha! Now I get it. All this is a pathetic attempt to frighten me out. And pathetic's the word. You should have taken a lesson or two from that old crack-pot Parry.
Nan (*furious*) Oh, if only she could hear me!
Hattie Be careful; you'll make them do something.
Mrs Coyle Good. Good! Make them do it. Go on, make them do it. I'm waiting.

Hattie looks round at the others

Bee Tell her to look at that shawl on the sofa.
Hattie Why?
Mrs Coyle Because it'll show how stupid your empty threats are.
Bee Go on, Hattie: the shawl.
Hattie (*to Mrs Coyle*) Look at that shawl.
Mrs Coyle Why should I look at a tuppenny-halfpenny grubby old shawl?
Bee (*indignantly*) My husband brought that back from Peking. It's all hand-embroidered and worth a lot of money.
Brigadier Watch it, you old cow.
Hattie (*to Mrs Coyle*) Watch it, you old cow. (*Then realizing what's she said she covers her lips*) I mean: I do think we'd better watch it.
Mrs Coyle (*heavily sarcastic*) All right, then. I'm watching. So what?

As she and Hattie watch Bee moves it very slightly

(*Drawing back a little*) That's odd. I thought I saw it move.
Hattie It did move.
Mrs Coyle It can't have. I know this flat's as draughty as a lighthouse ...
Bee (*indignantly*) It's nothing of the sort.
Mrs Coyle But I wouldn't have thought actually strong enough to move anything as heavy as that. No, of course it didn't move. It's because it's getting so dark in here; we must put on the lights. It can't possibly have moved.

Act II, Scene 2

Brigadier Watch again, soldier.
Hattie (*to Mrs Coyle*) Watch again, soldier. I mean watch again.

Bee lifts it slowly, moves it in a slight circle, then spreads it out again

Mrs Coyle (*for the first time unsure*) It did move.
Hattie (*eagerly*) It did, didn't it. I told you the place was haunted: there you are.
Mrs Coyle But it can't have. It's quite impossible. You've influenced me somehow. Perhaps sniffing that drug bottle. It's made me imagine things. (*Unconvincingly*) Of course it didn't move.
Nan Go on give it a good whirl, Dame Beatrice. Convince her.

Bee floats the shawl round the room to the growing horror of Mrs Coyle

Mrs Coyle (*when the shawl is settled on the sofa again*) It's a trick. It must be a trick. Are you doing this?
Hattie You saw: I was just sitting here.
Mrs Coyle But shawls don't just float about.
Nan Let me have a go: I'll show the old harridan. Tell her to watch.
Hattie They say you're to watch.
Mrs Coyle (*getting really frightened*) The Voices?
Hattie (*nodding*) The Voices.
Mrs Coyle (*turning her head away so that she can't see the shawl*) Well, I'm not going to. It's quite absurd. Quite impossible. (*But she waits in apprehension*)

Nan takes up the shawl, floats it towards her, and tickles her ear with the fringe. Mrs Coyle turns and sees it, and rising, watches in horror as Nan speeds round the room with it. Then stops suddenly, and drawing it into a long "snake" slowly wiggles it through the air towards the appalled Mrs Coyle

Hattie (*cheerfully*) I think it's after you.
Mrs Coyle (*backing away*) It can't be—it can't be.
Hattie It looks very determined.

Nan stands swaying the "snake's head" in front of her face

Hattie I think it's going to attack you.
Mrs Coyle It is. It is! Miss Hatfield, stop it, stop it!
Bee Perhaps it will stop if she agrees to go back to her flat.
Hattie (*to Mrs Coyle*) Perhaps it will stop if you agree to go back to your flat.
Mrs Coyle (*getting slightly hysterical*) No, I won't. I know it's all an hallucination. I will not be bullied by voices and snakes——

Nan starts the "snake" towards her neck. Mrs Coyle is completely terrified

Help! It's going to strangle me. I don't believe in it, but it's going to strangle me. No, I refuse to believe it's happening. I refuse. But I do think—(*her voice rising to a scream*)—I'll just go to my bedroom for a moment.

She flees from the room

Brigadier A few brief visits to her bedroom tonight, and I'll guarantee she'll be back in her own flat in the morning.
Hattie Oh, thank you so much.
Nan And if she doesn't behave we'll haunt her out of that, too.
Hattie I can't tell you how grateful I am. Oh, it's all so exciting. Tell me about what it's like where you are.
Bee Careful. Someone coming.

Mrs Honeywell comes in with a tray and proceeds to put the tea-things on it

Mrs Honeywell What's the matter with Mrs Coyle? Looked as if she'd seen a ghost.
Hattie She did?
Mrs Honeywell All that hot buttered toast having an effect, I expect. But I was determined she shouldn't have your quince jam.
Hattie Thank you.
Nan Shall we have a little fun with her?
Bee No, she's been so good in supporting Hattie.
Brigadier It was all her fault of course.
Bee Yes. Well, just a little.
Hattie Oh, I don't think you should.
Mrs Honeywell (*turning to her*) What, Miss Hattie, dear?

During this dialogue Nan silently unloads the tray and puts all the things back on the table

Hattie Oh, did I say something?
Mrs Honeywell Yes, you said you didn't think you should.
Hattie Did I? Now I wonder why I said that?
Mrs Honeywell Because you missed your tea, I expect. I'll make you a fresh pot. (*Turning to the table*) If you take it with a nice aspirin——(*She breaks off as she sees her tray is empty. She stares, and shakes her head disbelievingly*) I could have sworn I packed up the tray . . .
Hattie It's difficult to see. I think we'd better light up early.
Mrs Honeywell OK.

She goes to the door. But as she puts her hand out to the switch the Brigadier turns the light on. Mrs Honeywell stands very puzzled

I think I'm getting double vision.
Hattie Perhaps you'd better see the oculist.
Mrs Honeywell (*going to the table lamp*) Yes, I think.

But as she puts her hand to it Bee turns it on. Mrs Honeywell is really upset

Do I look all right, dear?
Hattie A little pale, but otherwise all right.
Mrs Honeywell Well, I don't think I am.

She goes to the tray. It has been repacked by Nan. Mrs Honeywell goes to replace things, and is again staggered

Act II, Scene 2

(*Eventually*) I'm sure I'm not. (*She takes up the tray*) I'm certainly going to give up gin.

She hurries out

Hattie It's a shame.
Bee (*laughing*) Yes, it is. Sell my telephone shares and give her a rise in salary.
Brigadier (*busily*) Enough frivolity. We must get to work.
Nan (*to Hattie*) And tell you the real purpose for coming back.
Bee So, dear, gather up all your strength and ingenuity...
Hattie That won't take long.
Brigadier And pay careful attention. You'd better sit down.

She sits, and they all draw up chairs round her

Now: our Peak of Happiness idea turned out to be brilliant.
Nan So much so that we don't want it wasted.
Bee There are masses of people it would help quite enormously.
Brigadier (*slowly and clearly*) So, we've decided you shall carry on.
Hattie Me! Alone! (*Horrified*) But I couldn't. I couldn't possibly!
Nan Of course you can.
Hattie I couldn't!
Brigadier We shall plan it all...
Bee See you through every stage of it...
Nan And be with you all the time.
Hattie But I couldn't do it. I know I couldn't. Surely there's someone else?
Bee No; we're only allowed to work through you.
Brigadier So concentrate on what I'm going to say. (*Consulting his clipboard*) We want you to start with a nice dentist who has a practice in——
Hattie (*interrupting frantically*) Oh, not a dentist, please! I only have to think of one and I tremble. Please not a dentist.
Nan All right: we'll postpone the dentist.
Hattie No, no, cancel the appointment altogether.
Brigadier (*crossing out crossly*) Very well. We'll go on to Mrs X.
Bee You'll love her: she's a sweet, charming and altogether delightful woman married to a complete crook...
Nan Whom she loves too much to realize.
Brigadier His business is about to go bust; and the cad's going to make a bunk abroad with a rich widow he's charmed.
Nan Which will leave Mrs X not only completely heart-broken, but loaded with debts.
Hattie (*pitifully*) Then where's the peak of happiness?
Brigadier It's their silver wedding next Saturday. To cover his tracks he's giving her a party. She's never allowed one, so is especially thrilled.
Nan On the night of the party he'll be charming to her as he wants her to sign something. She'll be so delighted that——Damn—someone coming.

Dolores, with a new hair-do, comes in

Dolores Hi, Hattie.

Hattie Oh, hello, Dolores.
Dolores Only two secs as one of my client's kids has nits. But I thought I must pop in and tell you the good news.
Hattie What?
Dolores Chuck and I are going to be married.
Bee Oh, how splendid! I'm delighted.
Hattie Dame Beatrice is delighted. (*Correcting hastily*) Would have been delighted. And so am I. Many congratulations.
Bee We must give her a wedding present.
Dolores Oh, thank you.
Hattie (*astonished*) You heard?
Dolores I was thanking you for your congratulations.
Hattie Oh, yes.
Bee You know my secret hiding-place for my only good brooch?

Hattie nods

Give it to her with our love.
Hattie All right. (*She goes to the curtains, and unpins the brooch*)
Dolores (*watching her in astonishment*) Are you all right?
Hattie (*approaching Dolores*) Dame Beatrice wants you to have this.
Dolores I don't understand. Dame Beatrice?
Hattie Was very fond of you. And I know wanted you to have it when you married. (*Giving it*) So it's from all of us.
Dolores But I couldn't.
Brigadier Tell her to take it and buzz off to her nits.
Hattie You're to take it and buzz off to the nits. Please.
Dolores It's terribly generous. I'll come back and thank you properly on my way back. (*Kissing her*) But thanks ever so, ever so; ever so.

She goes out

Brigadier Now come along, come along; we'll be called back before you're fully briefed. (*To Hattie*) Are you clear so far?
Hattie No.
Nan (*comfortingly*) I'll come early on the day, and run through it with you alone.
Bee We think it'd be silly to do it in this flat again ...
Hattie That I do understand; and completely agree.
Brigadier So we've planned it in the Xs' house.
Hattie I don't suppose I should even be able to find it!
Bee You go by taxi so he'll find it.
Brigadier The only slightly ticklish part is the actual—dismissal. Where's the stuff?
Hattie Where I rehid it from the police.
Nan You were very clever about that.
Brigadier Get it, will you?
Hattie Can't we leave it where it is till Saturday?
Nan We've got to rehearse the tricky bit.
Brigadier (*in his best military manner*) Fetch it, Hatfield.

Act II, Scene 2

Hattie (*rushing to fetch it, giving a vague salute*) Oh, yes, sir; I'm so sorry... (*She climbs on a chair and takes down a large vase. Removes a smaller vase from inside. From this she takes out an old coffee-tin out of which she produces a packet of tea. She pours this out on the table and unearths a small parcel wrapped in tin-foil. She shows the tablets inside*)

Brigadier Good. Running a bit short. (*To Nan*) Remind me to consult how to get more when we get back. (*To Hattie*) Now—the actual wine hasn't been ordered yet. But the object's the same whatever it is: to get one of these into the celebration glass at the critical moment.

Bee And of course you must do it unseen.

Hattie (*making up her mind*) It'll be unseen all right. Because I'm not going to do it.

Bee You are going to do it, Hattie dear.

Hattie Just the thought of it's making me feel peculiar.

Nan If you let us down we may not be allowed to come again.

Hattie Oh, you must! You can't desert me. Please! All right, I'll try. But do explain it terribly simply.

Brigadier We will. It's really an old trick that the conjurors used to use. (*Pointing to Hattie's tonic glass*) Put that as the celebration glass. And we'll practise till you could do it in your sleep.

Hattie (*pitifully*) I don't suppose I shall ever sleep again.

Brigadier Now. Take a pill between your thumb and first finger of your left hand.

Hattie dithers

Come along, come along.

Hattie stretches out her right hand

Left hand, Hatfield!

Hattie But I'm right-handed; I could never manage anything with my left hand.

Nan You're only using it to pick up the pill; you immediately transfer it to the right hand.

Hattie Then why don't I pick it up with my right hand straight away?

Brigadier (*with monumental patience*) Because, Miss Hatfield, we have taken pains to work out a system that is fool-proof. (*More to himself*) Or so we thought.

Bee Trust us, dear. Start again quietly and calmly.

Hattie (*doing so*) Take a pill up with my left hand.

Brigadier Splendid. Now, hold it there while you turn your other hand— your right hand—palm upwards.

She does so

Good. Now pass the pill over to the palm hand, and hold it firmly there in the crease. (*Demonstrating*) Now, turn the right hand palm downwards.

Hattie does so, and drops the pill

(*Furious*) I said hold it there!

Hattie (*picking it up*) Oh, I am so sorry.
Nan Quite natural your first time. But it's really not difficult.
Bee I've got smaller hands than you, and found it quite easy every time. I'll do it with you, dear.
Nan We all will.
Brigadier Now, start again. Pick pill up with left hand.

Hattie takes up the pill as the others mime to the Brigadier's instructions

Transfer to right palm. Hold tight. Turn palm over. Pass hand over glass as if taking potato-crisp from other side. Release pill when exactly over glass.

They all open their hands. As does Hattie. Her pill falls in the glass

Bravo!
Bee Perfect first time.
Hattie (*pleased*) It wasn't really as difficult as I expected.
Brigadier That's the spirit. But I think we'll try it at least once more. Take a pill with the left hand——
Nan (*interrupting*) Wait a moment—someone coming.
Hattie (*panicking*) It's Mrs Coyle. She'll find out and tell the police. (*She hides the pills under a cushion*)
Bee No, it's not her. It's one of us.

Fay, also looking ethereal, appears

Hattie Fay! Are you all right?
Fay Darling, it's absolutely heaven! Well, strictly speaking, not exactly that, yet. But they're such darlings one's full of hope. And it really is blissful. I'm sublimely happy. So I thought I must just come and thank you.
Hattie Thank me?
Fay Well, you did help, my little cabbage. And actually there was something else most important I wanted to find out.
Hattie Yes?
Fay (*urgently*) How's my play going?
Hattie Oh, it came off after only three performances.
Fay (*clasping her hands*) Joy eternal, a flop! (*Looking up*) I don't mind if it does earn me bad points, but that is the most satisfactory and sustaining news I've heard since I was christened! Glorious. Can't wait to tell the other actresses. Bye, my darling.

She disappears

Brigadier (*crossly*) I checked her schedule: she wasn't due to come here this afternoon.
Bee She does so love making appearances.
Brigadier Very inconsiderate. It means we'll have to cut corners and hurry. Now. Listen very carefully, Hatfield.
Hattie I think I'm beyond it.
Brigadier Rubbish. You order a taxi to fetch you at twenty-two hundred hours Saturday next.

Act II, Scene 2

Hattie You promised you'd put it simply!
Nan Ten o'clock, dear.
Hattie (*aghast*) Ten o'clock at night!?
Brigadier The party only starts at twenty-one hundred.
Hattie But I can't possibly stay up till ten o'clock at night! I'm always in bed at half-past nine.
Bee You must have a nice rest in the afternoon instead.
Brigadier Immediately you get to the party——
Hattie (*frantically*) No, no, I can't get there; I can't really. The thought of a party absolutely terrifies me. I haven't been to one for years and years. I couldn't possibly arrive alone.
Nan We shall be there, dear.
Hattie (*working herself into a state*) But I shan't be able to talk to you! I can't be seen speaking to the—unknown in the middle of a milling throng. I'll feel lost and embarrassed—no-one will talk to me—I'll look peculiar—I've nothing to wear——
Bee That nice dress Dolores brought.
Hattie Oh, yes. But what's the use of looking nice in the middle of a milling throng who aren't talking to you? (*Getting frantic again*) Except probably to ask what I'm doing there! And I shan't know what to say! And they'll find out I'm an impostor. And they'll call the police——
Nan For mercy's sake don't bring the police in.
Hattie (*getting more and more worked up*) They'll come in by themselves! And they'll arrest me. And I shall be grilled! And I'll never be able to withstand them. I shall crack under grilling——
Nan Now, calm down, old girl.
Hattie I can't calm down. They'll grill me, and find out exactly what happened to you all and Fay. And I shall be accused! And before I know where I am I shall be in the dock at the Old Bailey!
Brigadier Take it easy, Miss Hatfield, take it easy.
Hattie (*becoming hysterical*) It's all very well you floating about saying take it easy! You wouldn't if you were down here being pointed at by a judge in a black cap. And with my picture being splashed all over the front pages. And popping up every news on the television. And reporters pushing machines at me, and shouting through the letter-box——
Bee Now, be sensible, Hattie——
Hattie (*almost incomprehensible*) I'm past being sensible! I'm falling to pieces. Look! I'm one big tremble. And I'm not even in the middle of the milling throng yet. What shall I be like when I'm there trying to palm pills into glasses? Look at my hands! They're shaking so now I couldn't even pick up a potato crisp. (*Almost shrieking*) What'll I be like at the Peak Party? Even worse! Only I couldn't be even worse. My heart's jumping like a road-mender's thing. And everything's going round, and round, and round, and round. Quickly: I must stop it, I must stop it! Nerve-tonic—nerve-tonic . . .

Before they can stop her she seizes up her glass, and swallows the rest of the contents. And immediately falls to the floor

During this, the Lights have dimmed, and the others disappeared Bagpipes are heard faintly in the distance. Then, from above:

Bee's voice How lovely, Hattie. Welcome, my dear, welcome!
Nan's voice Marvellous to have you with us, old girl!
Brigadier's voice What a perfectly splendid surprise, Miss Hatfield.
Fay's voice What utter bliss that you've joined us, my little cabbage.
All four voices Welcome, welcome, welcome ...

Their continued greetings are drowned by the bagpipes in full blast

CURTAIN

FURNITURE AND PROPERTY LIST

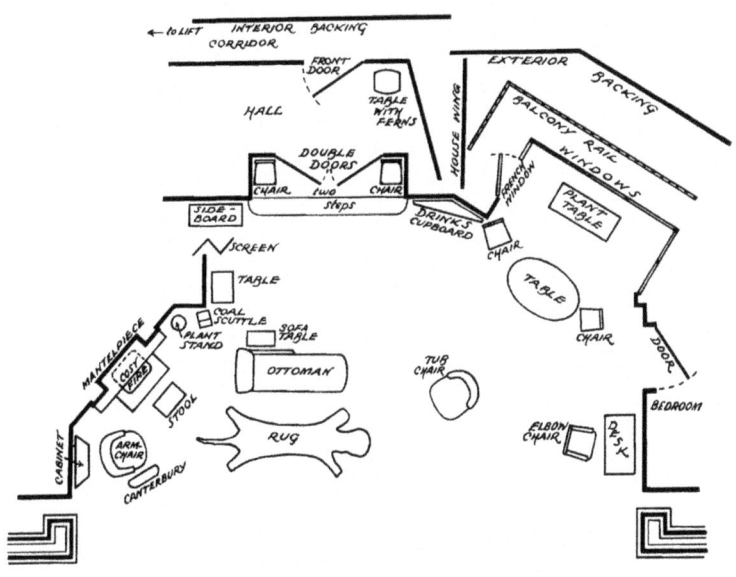

ACT I

Scene 1

On stage: Desk. *On it:* table lamp, telephone, address book, paper, envelopes, pens
Desk chair
Waste-paper basket
Dining-table with flaps
4 upright chairs
Table with plants. *On it:* pair of binoculars
Sideboard
Grandfather clock
Small table. *On it:* table lamp, gramophone. *Under it:* records
Fireplace. *In it:* stove. *By it:* coal scuttle, poker
Stool
Plant stand
Sofa. *On it:* cushions, large embroidered shawl

Sofa table. *On it:* hand-bell, Dolores' bag and hairdressing apparatus—curlers, brushes, etc.
2 armchairs
Cabinet. *In it:* china
On wall: house phone
Carpet
Rug
Window curtains (open)
Various ornaments
In hall: table with plants
Other dressing as required

Off stage: Clip-board with pen **(Brigadier)**
Tray with five mugs of coffee **(Mrs Honeywell)**
2-handled straw basket with bit of blanket **(Mrs Coyle)**
Identical straw basket **(Hattie)**
Small tin of pills **(Brigadier)**
Small tub chair **(Bee** and **Nan)**
2nd tub chair **(Nan)**
1st tub chair with basket **(Nan)**
2nd tub chair with basket **(Nan)**
Vase **(Brigadier)**

Personal: **Brigadier:** wrist-watch (required throughout)
Hattie: handkerchief with knot

Scene 2

Strike: 2nd tub-chair, basket
Tray and mugs
Vase

Re-set: Waste-paper basket by desk

Set: Tablecloth on table, plus lunch settings for 6, including 6 small plates, 6 dinner plates, napkins, glasses, serving spoons, carving knife, dish of horse-radish
4 upright chairs round table
Desk chair near sofa
Script for **Nan**
Carrier-bag with 2 bottles of champagne by sofa
Tray with bottle of sherry and glasses on sofa table
Bottle of nerve-tonic and glass on small table
Dish of mousse on sideboard

Off stage: Small vase of flowers **(Hattie)**
Bundle wrapped up in blanket **(Mrs Coyle)**
Dog basket **(Hattie)**
Tub chair with other basket hidden behind cushion **(Nan)**
Tray with joint of roast beef, dishes of vegetables, potatoes, Yorkshire pudding, gravy **(Mrs Honeywell)**
Opened bottle of claret **(Brigadier)**
Shawl concealing dog basket **(Nan)**

Winter Glory

ACT II

Scene 1

Strike: All dishes, cutlery, glasses, food, bottles of wine, tablecloth, etc. from dining-table
Carrier-bag and bottles of champagne
Tray with bottle of sherry and glasses
Fay's script
Tub chair
Basket
Small vase of flowers

Re-set: Dining-table and 3 chairs in original positions
Desk chair at desk
Shawl draped over sofa

Check: Bottle of nerve-tonic and glass on small table

Set: Chair C for **Hattie**
Box of pins for **Nan**
Box of lace and ribbons and feathers for **Bee**
Newspaper
Brigadier's clip-board and pen on desk
Bottle of champagne in sideboard
Small tin of pills in bottom of ornament

Off stage: Cardboard box with long dress **(Dolores)**
Tray with 5 glasses of champagne, only 1 glass fully filled **(Mrs Honeywell)**
Long rolled-up carpet **(Sergeant Waller** and **Bert)**

Scene 2

Strike: Box with dress, box of pins, box of lace and ribbons
Tray and champagne glasses
Newspaper, **Brigadier**'s clip-board

Check: Bottle of nerve-tonic and glass on small table

Set: Tea laid out on table, including cups and saucers, pot of tea, toast, etc.
Hand-bell on table
Brooch pinned to curtains
Small tin-foil parcel of pills in packet of tea, inside old coffee-tin, inside small vase, inside large vase on top of cabinet

Off stage: Plate of toast, pot of jam **(Mrs Honeywell)**
Clip-board and pen **(Brigadier)**
Tray **(Mrs Honeywell)**

LIGHTING PLOT

Practical fittings required: 2 table lamps, pendant
Interior. A drawing-room. The same scene throughout

ACT I, SCENE 1. Morning
To open: General interior lighting
No cues

ACT 1, SCENE 2 Early afternoon
To open: General interior lighting
No cues

ACT II, SCENE 1 Afternoon
To open: General interior lighting
No cues

ACT II, SCENE 2 Afternoon

Cue 1	**Brigadier** turns on pendant *Snap on pendant*	(Page 54)
Cue 2	**Bee** turns on table lamp *Snap on table lamp*	(Page 54)
Cue 3	As **Hattie** falls to the floor *Dim lights*	(Page 59)

EFFECTS PLOT

Please read the notice on page 66 concerning the use of copyright music and commercial recordings

ACT I

Cue 1	Shortly after CURTAIN rises *Telephone rings*	(Page 1)

ACT II

Cue 2	**Bee** (*calling*): "... when she arrives." *House phone rings*	(Page 41)
Cue 3	**Fay:** "... heal my tattered nerves." *Music: Funeral March*	(Page 43)
Cue 4	**Bee** stops record *Cut music*	(Page 43)
Cue 5	**Bee:** "Let's have the other." *Music*	(Page 43)
Cue 6	**Bee** turns off record *Cut music*	(Page 43)
Cue 7	As **Fay** falls out of sight into bedroom *Crash of glass*	(Page 44)
Cue 8	**Hattie** sinks slowly back into chair *Distant sound of bagpipes—fade as voices speak as script page 46*	(Page 46)
Cue 9	As SCENE 2 opens *Banal music from gramophone*	(Page 46)
Cue 10	**Mrs Honeywell** (*acidly*): "Thanks." (*She starts to go to the door*) *Music ends*	(Page 47)
Cue 11	**Hattie:** "I don't know what to do." *Faint sounds of bagpipes*	(Page 49)
Cue 12	**Mrs Coyle:** "... nothing to hear." *Bagpipes become louder*	(Page 50)
Cue 13	**Mrs Coyle:** "... at the Edinburgh Tattoo again?" *Fade bagpipes slightly as voices speak*	(Page 50)
Cue 14	**Brigadier's voice:** "... on parade troops." *Bagpipes blare out*	(Page 51)
Cue 15	**Bee:** "... in the meantime?" *Toot on bagpipes, then they stop*	(Page 51)
Cue 16	After **Hattie** falls to the floor *Bagpipes faintly in distance, then voices as script page 60, followed by bagpipes in full blast*	(Page 59)

A licence issued by Samuel French Ltd to perform this play does not include permission to use the Incidental music specified in this copy. Where the place of performance is already licensed by the Performing Right Society a return of the music used must be made to them. If the place of performance is not so licensed then application should be made to the PERFORMING RIGHT SOCIETY, 29 Berners Street, London W1.

A separate and additional licence from PHONOGRAPHIC PERFORMANCES LTD, Ganton House, Ganton Street, London W1, is needed whenever commercial recordings are used.

www.ingramcontent.com/pod-product-compliance
Ingram Content Group UK Ltd.
Pitfield, Milton Keynes, MK11 3LW, UK
UKHW021846210426
5322IPUK00022B/505